Reclaiming India

Views of Public Intellectuals

Reclaiming India
Views of Public Intellectuals

Compiled by
Shabnam Hashmi & Leena Dabiru

frontpage

frontpage
https://frontpagepublications.com

First published 2023

Frontpage Publications Limited
Level 2, 13 John Prince's Street, London W1G 0JR, United Kingdom

Frontpage Publications USA LLC
29 Van Buren Ave, Unit I-8, Norwalk, CT 06850, USA

Frontpage
Level B, 76 B B Ganguly Street, Kolkata 700012, India

British Library Cataloguing in Publishing Data
A Catalogue record for this book is available from the British Library

ISBN: 978 93 81043 58 5

Printed & bound in India by Atlantic Print Services

Typeset by Sonal Mansata
85 Park Street, Kolkata 700016, India

Contents

Contributors

ABIRAMI JOTHEESWARAN, General Secretary, All India Dalit Mahila Adhikar Manch, Delhi

ADITYA MUKHERJEE, Professor of Contemporary History (Retired), Jawaharlal Nehru University, Delhi

ANAND PATWARDHAN, Filmmaker

ANJALI BHARDWAJ, Social Activist

ASHOK VAJPEYI, Poet-Critic and Art Lover

D RAJA, General Secretary, Communist Party of India, Former Member of Parliament

DHRUV RAINA, Professor, Zakir Husain Centre for Educational Studies, Jawaharlal Nehru University, Delhi

ENAKSHI GANGULY, Child Rights Activist, Co-Founder, HAQ: Centre for Child Rights, Delhi

GAUTAM MENON, Professor, Ashoka University, Sonepat

HARTOSH SINGH BAL, Political Editor, *The Caravan*, Delhi

K SRINATH REDDY, President, Public Health Foundation of India, Delhi

MOGALLAN BHARTI, Political Scientist

MRIDULA MUKHERJEE, Professor of Modern History (Retired), Jawaharlal Nehru University, Delhi

NIVEDITA MENON, Professor, Jawaharlal Nehru University, Delhi

PRASHANT BHUSHAN, Public Interest Lawyer & Activist

ROMILA THAPAR, Professor Emerita, Jawaharlal Nehru University, Delhi

S IRFAN HABIB, Historian of Science and of Modern Political History

SHASHI THAROOR, Member of Lok Sabha

SUKUMAR MURALIDHARAN, Media Professional

TEHMINA ARORA, Lawyer

TM KRISHNA, Vocalist, Writer and Activist

Foreword

The idea of India, that much-debated concept, is more contested than ever before. Rabid bigotry and viciously lowbrow communal jibes overwhelm public discourse, and the kind of 'othering' Indians would have once abhorred is now, apparently, common-or-garden political rhetoric. Thoughts that it would have been deemed inappropriate to express even behind closed doors are now routinely declaimed from political platforms. Our institutions are faltering, our freedoms feel more and more circumscribed, and more important, we are falling painfully short of the high ideals we dedicated ourselves to through the civic nationalism of our national movement.

The 'argumentative Indian' of Amartya Sen's famous formulation has become raucous and bigoted in the social media age. The availability of instant gratification has made her tribalistic, compromising her ability to listen, learn and evolve. The current moment beckons the question—are we satisfied with the quality of discourse we see around us today? No Indian proud of their longstanding tradition of pluralism and heterodoxy will answer that today with a resounding yes.

India is the land of Adi Shankara and Charvaka, Kabir and Basavanna, Akbar and Raja Rammohun Roy—and Indians are the inheritors of a civilizational heritage that encouraged dissent and diversity of opinion. The delicate balance Indian constitutionalism struck between individual and community identity, awarding extensive civil liberties and democratic rights to a hitherto subjugated people, was meant to nurture this heritage. By creating a republic committed to liberty, equality and fraternity, the founders of our Republic were mortgaging our future to our fulfilment of a crucial responsibility—that we would continue to respond to the contingencies of politics with the same self-possession and moral sensitivity as they did.

The least we owe them, whatever be our political views, is a commitment to uphold a discourse that is constructive and respectful, rather than a cacophony of noisy invective which drowns out all nuanced and reasoned debate. This is precisely where the 'Reimagining India' lecture series nestles itself. The chapters in this book must not be viewed as 'lectures' in the conventional, classroom sense. They are much more; they are conversations, filled with the exploration of the foundational ideas we seem to have forgotten. These are engagements that go to the very heart of India's spirit—an exemplary model of the kind of discourse we need to inculcate.

What you are going to encounter in the following pages is going to be an eclectic mix of perspectives. Poet and art critic Ashok Vajpeyi will call upon you to safeguard India's cultural pluralism. Activist Anjali Bhardwaj will teach you the fundamentals of participatory democracy through the safeguarding and instrumentalisation of the Right to Information. Romila Thapar will enlighten you to the spirit of dissent encoded in our history, while Prashant Bhushan will ask you to reclaim the republic's dwindling essence.

The 21 credible voices in this book are not repetitive or uniform in their logic, either. They are a spectrum of diverse perspectives, each unique in its own right, and some even conflicting with others. The credo of this volume lies in its initiative to transcend the politico-social sphere to cover all aspects of civil society. You will find here K Srinath Reddy's roadmap to revamp our healthcare system to make it more equitable, just a few pages apart from Gautam Menon's vision for Indian science. Creative freedom, censorship, rights of minorities, musical heritage, feminism, and economics are all interestingly interwoven into a series that stands true to the invaluable spirit of debate and civic engagement.

You may not agree with everyone in this volume. You may, for instance, disagree with my evaluation of Mr Modi's foreign policy, penned a couple of years ago. Or, agree with some points and strongly disagree with others. You may even have your own reasoned counter-arguments. And that is the very beauty of this process—you'd have heard me out, disagreed with my point of view, and gone a long way in developing your own viewpoint. You'd have learnt to agree with me on the only thing that matters—the ground rules of how we disagree.

In a world where the Twitter-troll mentality of perverse and pettily offensive insults now so deeply pervades our public life that we seem to have lost the ability to listen to those who do not conform to our views, this is a crucial intervention. Those who subscribe to the 'TINA' (There Is No Alternative) narrative to the way things have become, should read the following pages with an open mind to see how today's India can be reimagined. Even if you do not change your minds, you are likely to have expanded your intellectual horizons, and perhaps learned to challenge your assumptions through the logic, facts and sharp arguments contained in these lectures. By making you listen and think, the lecture-essays in this volume will have served their purpose.

Those of us who aspire for the India that Mahatma Gandhi, Nehru, or Ambedkar imagined and expected us to foster are desperately searching for a palliative to today's epidemic of hate. I have always called India a country that is much more than the sum of its parts. In my experience, that is the most frequently proven truism about our country. Those who peruse this volume are likely to experience it for themselves, for *Reclaiming India* affirms it with great poise and conviction.

SHASHI THAROOR
July 2023

Cultural Pluralism

Safeguarding Cultural Pluralism

Ashok Vajpeyi

When we talk about India in cultural terms, we all too often forget that India is one of the world's few old civilisations world has seen. Not only are we one of the few civilisations, but we are a living civilisation, unlike many civilisations that have been buried in history, such as the Mayans, Romans, and Athenians.

This also means that India is one civilisation with several cultures. India has many cultures, not just one, which means that the country has over four thousand six hundred sociologically definable communities, over seven hundred languages and dialects, eight living religions, several forms of costumes and cuisines, and hundreds of customs. All this come together to constitute the mind-boggling plurality called India.

It is not for nothing, that in some countries of the West, India is a Plural Noun 'Indies', not simply India. Now, culture plays an important role in the life of people apart from embodying its material ambitions, it also embodies its spiritual dimensions metaphysical and philosophical concerns, and surely India too has this in abundance.

One of the factors which has to be noted that India is not only plural; nothing is allowed in India to remain singular for long time. Every Singularity ultimately turns into Plurality. So the idea of one language, one religion, one set of rules, etc just does not hold good in India. We have seen over the centuries that India has had eight religions. Four religions were invented in India—Hinduism, Buddhism, Jainism, and Sikhism. And four came from outside Islam, such as Christianity, Judaism, and others. Each of these religions has contributed greatly in art and architecture, in metaphysics and philosophy, in spirituality, in music, in theatre, in visual arts, in literature, etc.

So the Indian plurality is also a cultural plurality and it is also a creative plurality. It also works interaction and openness to each other. It could be said Indians as a culture, a civilisation; let me go back to my earlier postulate that India is a civilisation, it was a civilisation which accommodated plurality, accommodated the plurality of visions, of anxiety, of values, of costumes, of colour and what you have. So it is not merely plural, it is open and accommodating. Also Religions, religious communities, social communities, ethnic communities, they have all been interacting with each other and learning from each other.

There was a study conducted by two hundred social scientists, which arrived at the conclusion that India has four thousand six hundred or more communities, and not one of them could claim to be racially pure. So from this one can conclude that India is ceaseless celebration of racial impurities. So nothing is pure. In India, all notions of purity, whether in language, in religion, or in conduct behaviour, etc, seem completely irrelevant to the civilizational enterprise, which India is.

Now, culture, or more exact in terms of India, cultures in India are created, nurtured, changed, reformed by people. It is the people who create culture. The state has a very limited role; if you had to think in terms of percentages, 90% of cultures are created, reformed, changed, practised and nourished by people, and only 10% falls in the lap of the State, and that too by way of providing infrastructure and by way of institutional framework. And it is these infrastructures and these kinds of institutional facilities, which have been seriously damaged in last decade or so. They have been undermined, they have been undervalued, and they have become adjuncts of State, whereas for the number of years or decades in our republic they enjoyed autonomy but that autonomy now seemed to be a thing of the past.

So, one of the things that will have to be done is to come back and give cultures and cultural institutions their autonomy. Secondly, what is contained in culture, is incredible corpus of knowledge, visions, ideas, critical insights, works of imagination, thoughts about language, meaning, sexuality, drama, music, dance, literature, spirituality, liberation, morality, conduct, faith, philosophy, logic, arguments, contestations, dialogues and debates, meta physics, and a lot of every day wisdom.

All this has been in constant dialogue, and argumentation. Unfortunately, these days we are given to understand as if debate, dissent, disagreement, etc are things that have come to us from outside, that they do not belong to the Indian cultural ethos which is not true.

Look at all the great works the foundational works of the Indian civilisation right from the *Vedas* to the *Upanishads* to the *Mahabharata* and the *Ramayana* and to the other philosophical traditions, all of them raise questions, debates, all of them do not feel shy of dissent, they allow disagreement, in fact they respect dissent. So in a manner of speaking, India's spiritual heritage, its intellectual and moral heritage, it's a creative heritage, all together create a democratic ethos which we have now, 70 years ago made into the Constitution for India. That's what it is.

Therefore, we must not forget that the Constitution merely, if not merely, substantially incorporates the Indian traditions of plurality, accommodation, openness, interaction, dialogue, debate, disagreement etc. It is the Constitution, which gives us the freedom in a legal sense to disagree with the states of power that be. It is the Constitution that as I said moral, intellectual and philosophical traditions of India, which have all been created by the various religions and other factors which have come into making of India that we enjoy these freedoms. Now what is happening, however, is that culture is being reduced to spectacle to a bit of *tamasha*. There are important aspects of culture which have to be nourished, there is a vast archaeological, historical heritage which has to be taken care of. Their forms of creative expression which are in difficulties, especially after COVID-19, and all that has to be cared for. And therefore, we have to have an alternative vision.

And part of that alternative vision will be that you cannot possibly make India a religious civilisation in terms of a single religion. You have to survive as a civilisation only through what Gandhi ji called *Sarva Dharma Sambhav*, that is every religion will have a place and every religion would be respected; these ideas have to be encouraged and nourished.

What are these ideas? These are the ideas relating to plurality, accommodativeness, interaction, dialogue. These are the ideas which should have questioning spirit, interrogative spirit, which is sometimes called the scientific temper.

Now in more concrete terms how some of these ideas can be promoted:

1 Gram Panchayats have been kept out of the cultural map of India, as if they have nothing to do. Although it is in the grams and gram panchayats that a lot of culture takes place, survives and thrives. There are any number of archaeological monuments which are neither protected by the Archaeological Survey of India nor by the Archaeology Directorate of the State Governments. A single step could be taken that all archaeological or historical monuments falling within the jurisdiction of a gram panchayat should be transferred to the gram panchayats. They should own these monuments and take care of them. They would have to be trained, some funds would have to be provided, some kind of a manual of care, renovation and preservation will have to be provided. All that can be done. Our rural schools again are mostly located in places where cultures are found. But they are kept away from taking any part in the cultural life within the school. My suggestion would be that all schools, their teachers and their students should start collecting folk songs and other folk traditional material falling within their geography. And they should be made to feel proud of and concerned with the cultural richness of their neighbourhood, whether it is in terms of crafts, in terms of folk tales. These are very rich materials and they should be made to take care of that and also to feel proud of it. Each school must celebrate if not a day but a week

of mother tongues. You see the language in which they are taught in the school is a standard language. But the whole lot of dialects, which they speak at home, in the family or in the society at large, these dialects must be acknowledged within the presence of the school by celebrating a week as I suggest.

2 Residences, work places of important writers, artists, teachers and other intellectuals should be marked and communities and neighbourhood should encourage to keep them in good condition. In the last fifty years, India has produced by a simple assessment, perhaps a hundred of top celebrities in the world of music, theatre, cinema, dance, literature. What have we done to protect their places, their residences, the materials that they have left behind which can be very interesting and inspiring for others to see? I once saw that in England, there's a convention that a house in which some important person lived has a blue circle and it is marked so that people know that such person lived here.

There has to be at the state level a greater awareness of the broad and rich cultural heritage the state has. States have museums but not all of them have what I would call as state folk-art survey, something like the Archaeological Survey of India, there ought to be a folk-art survey of Madhya Pradesh or Uttar Pradesh.

Also there ought to be the Adivasi languages and literatures, they are now coming to fruition, many Adivasi language books are being published but there is no attempt to put these together, not necessarily in the conventional museum form, but in the more open ended, in a more tribal life kind of a form in which these should be preserved and they must be given due respect. Adivasis are not meant to dance around when a VIP is visiting and that's it. That's the most insulting form of respect if at all. They should be cared for and respected for what they are.

Each state has many languages, although there are linguistic states to tell. Andhra and Telangana will have Telugu, but there's also Urdu there, there's also Hindi there and there might be other dialects and border areas there will be a bit of Tamil, a bit of Malayalam or whatever. So each language territory is very porous. And this idea that our language is great but there are several neighbourhood languages which are also great should be stressed. And therefore a state museum of languages and literature should be set up.

Universities which are technical universities, there is such a huge stress, heavy stress on instrumentalisation of education that the broad liberal education is being given up. So we are going to produce Robots and persons who will have no idea, they will technically be perfect but with no idea of the world they are going to be thrown in after they finish their education.

So in IITs, technical universities, all universities there ought to be in engineering colleges, medical colleges, residencies created for writers, artists to be there and to mix with the student population, talk to them about other aspects of life that they should know while they graduate or post graduate in some technical or whatever subject.

I think one of the great movements that took place in the Medieval India was the Bhakti movement. It started from the south and gone up to the north and it enabled the lower castes, the lower crafts people to exercise their right of creative expression. So look at that period you have Kabir who is a weaver, you have Ravidas who is a cobbler, you have Namdev who is a tailor and such like. This was a great period, there was an interaction a Kabir in Benaras which is a Vatican City of Hinduism let's say, is able to question and make fun of both the pandits and the maulvis and makes both the *Vedas* and the *Kitaab* irrelevant for spirituality and democratises spirituality which was thought to be exclusive domain of let's say, the brahmins or the wise ones.

Now this is a great movement in history and I say we should celebrate it through out the country, intellectually, creatively in different ways because each state will have some great Bhakti poets. There are *Vachana* poets, there are *Sangam* poets, there are *Aluwas* and such likes and of course the *Bhakti* poets in the north.

Coming to the national level, if you come to India, I mean to Delhi the capital, you don't have a national museum of Indian literature and Indian languages, as I said there are more than seven hundred languages and their literatures being written. Even twenty six languages are recognised by the Sahitya Academy against twenty two recognised by the 8th Schedule of the Constitution, but there are many more languages.

Now somebody who wants to know what India is all about must be able to do so by visiting such a museum, a national museum of Indian literature and languages. That could have a Rabindra Nath Tagore room, it could have a room for Prem Chand or Nirala or Mir and Ghalib and what you have. I mean these are great figures by all accounts. So let us celebrate the great Indians not the fake Indians, not the ones who claim to be Indian although they deny all the values of which that India has stood so far.

There ought to be a National Commission of Indian Languages, you have National Commission of Minorities, National Commission of Human Rights, National Commission of Women, there ought to be a National Commission of Indian Languages. We ought to know what is happening in our languages in terms of education, in terms of jurisprudence, in terms of information technology, in terms of education etc. And the whole country should know what is happening with our languages and corrective measures should be taken to see that if there are any difficulties or impediments or inadequacies that they are corrected.

There ought to be a National Artists-Writers Welfare Fund. You see when it comes to display ourselves in the world, what is it that you show? The world over India is identified in the first place with Gandhi ji and Nehru, you utter the name, they will say, oh the country of Gandhi, they will immediately know that.

Secondly, your music, your classical music, your classical dance, your visual art, your miniature art, your great sculptures, Buddhist sculptures, Islamic architecture, all this is what you are known for. But the writers and the artists who are struggling today to make these things, all too often in old age suffer from medical problems and there is no welfare, social welfare scheme which covers them. So there ought to be National Artist-Writers Welfare Fund, from which people in indigent circumstances can draw assistance. This could be created by the central government, by contributing amounts, getting amounts from the state governments also from publishing houses, music companies, etc.

See one of the things that is going to happen very soon is that our classical arts, especially music and dance are now steeped in deep mediocrity, because we have done nothing to save the age old tradition of *Guru Sishaya Parampara.* We have created modern institutions, there was zeal for modernising everything, we have thrown away the system. The system has its own difficulties of course, some distortions, have also come in. But we can take care of them. There ought to be a national programme in which, let's say, in the first instance we identify a hundred *Gurus* wherever they are all over the country in music and dance and provide them assistance to train four or five chosen disciples within a period of four to five years. Even if fifty per cent of them do not amount to much in terms of performance abilities, we still have something like two hundred fifty people being produced, which would be quite a remarkable achievement if we can do that.

Also there ought to be welfare measures for craftsmen. We have a crafts museum in Delhi, but it's in bad shape. We are making big things, big roads, big this, big that, but life, my dear friends, survives through small things. Big things don't help ordinary people. Ordinary people want small things, small things within their domestic domain as it were. You see we need small things, small things which we can handle without expertise, without having to deal with in an awesome manner. And these small things are our crafts whether in our handmade crafts, textile and all these. And, we are known in the world for them and crafts are one of the largest export items that India is able to handle. Now these crafts and craftsmen have been in a terrible condition, they have not been paid enough attention. So what we need is the revival of the crafts and a scheme in which crafts are promoted including the craft of making instruments for classical music, for instance Sitar, Sarod, Sarangi, these are very difficult instruments to make.

Let's go back to the Great India of Small Things rather than Great India of Monumental Follies.

Indian Culture—Our Failure

T M Krishna

How does one describe the times we are living in? It seems precarious, uncertain, hateful, angry, dangerous. We seem to get up to noise and sleep to noise. The noise is not just coming from out there, from others. It's coming from within. There's clutter and there is rumbling and in all this, there is no learning. It's reactive. We somehow seem to be within this mess, trying to grapple with ideas of culture, ideas of who we are, identities. Who is that person? Who are they? Who is the outsider? Who belongs? These are everyday rumblings within us. These are everyday conversations we are having with our families based on newspaper reports, WhatsApp forwards, fake news, Twitter, etc.

This is the culture that we are living in. I'm calling it culture because it is a kind of culture and it's cutting across generations. It's cutting across society, genders, castes, and faiths. It's just that each person is at a different power position and hence, is either receiving the oppressive nature of what we are dishing out or is participating in the violence. We are now living in a culture of violence. So, how does one respond to it? It's important that we respond every day and say things that go beyond these divisive ideas.

We also have to seriously reflect about what do we mean by saying we are Indian? We say we are proud to be Indian. But what does it mean? Is it just one line within which we live? Is there an idea of India truly? Let's ask that question. Not just historically, but culturally. Is there an India within you and me? Is there an India within every citizen? Does every citizen feel as Indian as I feel or do they feel differently? Do they feel that they don't belong? These are all the contradictions that we have to face up to. I'm a musician. I have sung from the age of six. I sing a form of music—Carnatic music—that's supposed to epitomise the idea of Indian culture. I have been told this. I believed it and I still believe it in some ways. But what did I really represent? What is this culture? You know, we keep reading about India being the land of diverse culture. I myself call it a cradle, where multiple cultures came in, mingled, talked to each other, disagreed with each other.

There is this deeply sentimental description of India. And in order to battle today, we seem to be running back to sentimentality, back to nostalgia, back to calling out names like Kabir and say, that's India. But these are all half-truths, aren't they? Because India is always a complicated place. India is not a seamless, creaseless textile. It is messy. So, when we speak about Indian culture in the past, let's put some reality to it. Let's first agree that human beings are always human beings, and we will do what we always do. So when we are facing what we are facing today, we should not just be responding to today or the next two years, but we have to reflect upon the past and the present, because we need to think of the next two decades, because this has to change. The way we engage with culture has to change now. There's an urgency to it. So, what do we do with our past? Do we then say, the past is a horrible place where evil things happen?

Yes, evil things did happen. The past is a place where people were divided. Like today. The past was a place where as much as we sang beautiful songs, we also made sure some people couldn't sing songs. But isn't that contradiction really India? The existence of that contradiction, that existence of the most wonderful sayings from the wonderful sage and the saints of various faiths and the violent acts of some, the violent thoughts of some, the othering of people. So, as a person of music, sometimes when I sing a song, I am reflecting on the meaning of the song. What does it say about the past? What does it say about me? Am I about myself and about today? Am I, in a way, passing onto people who are listening to me, just one side, just one angle? How do we get multiple angles together? So, let's talk about cultures in a manner that is complex, that is unresolved. Let's ask the question—why is today so much more precarious than 20 years ago? What is different?

One, we live in times when the people in power, the establishment, is ensuring to its fullest capacity that we do not believe that each of us have to live together unless we belong to one way of living. Sometimes its networks operate and bruise people, kill people and abuse them. So, here we are, facing an establishment-based violence. This poison has gone into every one of us. None of us, including me, is saved from the poison. I think of somebody as an enemy. I think of somebody who doesn't agree with these ideas as somebody who has to be shut out, who has to be, as they say today, cancelled, because that's in my head, too. We have to face this disturbing truth within ourselves and for which I think liberals like me, or what we like to call ourselves, have to reflect about how liberal we've really been. And that's what I'm going to talk about. I'm not here to point fingers to people. I'm here to talk about my own failings, our own failings, because we don't talk about that. What have we missed? Have we missed anything? When we became independent in 1947, we made many promises to ourselves. I think India was born that day to be specific. Then what was before that? Was that not India? I'm not going into this myth of India being an eternal civilisation. No, this was a land that was not India. This was a land of culture, land of people.

But India happens in 1947 because that's when we resolved to decide who we want to be. Yes, that came from the past, but it was also a radical movement in the history of this part of the world. A radical moment because anybody who reads our Constitution, anybody who hears what people said in 1947, would realise that there was a distinct recognition that the past was a place from which we take inspiration. But the present or that moment was also a moment when we say we cannot accept certain things about our own past, that we are creating a new land, a beautiful new land that was going to embrace a very different culture. That, to me, is Indian culture. Within that comes in plurality and diversity. So, when we say we're a diverse land, every diversity we talk about must be under the umbrella of what I would call Indian Constitutional Culture. Well, is the Indian Constitution perfect? Of course, it is not perfect. It's, after all, written, rewritten, redrafted, changed by human beings. But there are certain essentials, certain callings, certain gifts that we give ourselves that are important to recognise today in these times. But what did we do? The truth of the matter is that the liberals of this country ignored some essential aspects of who we are as people. We can call ourselves a democratic culture. We can call ourselves, like I said, a Constitutional culture. But there are cultures within cultures. And some of those cultures have existed for centuries, for millennia.

They operate within the family. They operate within small communities. They operate in regions, in ethnicities. They operate in these little, little dimensions. And the fact is that the liberals were not willing to engage with certain aspects of this culture. One fundamental aspect that we have ignored is faith and religion. What has been our discourse, our dialogue with that inner urge? That urge to believe in something more powerful? Universal? Universal consciousness? God, an idol, an idea? What has been the liberal conversation with that? It's not enough if we say we embraced every culture, every faith and every religion. And it's not enough, like I said, to go back and name people of the past. What has been the contemporary liberal conversation with these complex ideas? Of course, I concede that many of these things are built within oppressive caste and social structures and that's what makes our conversation even more essential, even more important. So, we've just let faith happen. People who believed to do what they did. But what has been the democratic conversation with those worlds? And that's the major part of this country. Why does a person believe? Why is there faith? Because that is hope. That is hope that tomorrow somehow my day will be better when the sun rises that I may earn a few more rupees that my child may be able to go to school.

Hope is essential and faith gives people hope. How have we failed to connect these dots in the way we have spoken to ourselves and our society? But there is a problem. Where is the respect for faith within the liberal world? We have got to a point where we've allowed the idea of being liberal or progressive to be a synonym for atheism. But these are not connected at all. These are absolutely different ideas. So where is the progressive, theistic conversation? Where is the progressive, respectful conversation for ritual, for faith, for ways of living? Because it's very convenient for us, the social elites, to say, I separate religion from culture. I consider myself culturally Hindu or culturally Muslim, but not religiously. Come on, think about it. Isn't that privilege to be able to say that every other person who doesn't have this privilege connects the two? It's connected to their art, their song, their theatre, their faith, the space, everything is interlinked. So how does one pick holes and somehow separate those two things? You can't separate those two things. So how does one engage in a conversation with that? Have we? We have not.

That's something we have to think about very deeply. How does one build a conversation, a respectful, non-condescending conversation with people of faith? Because we are also judging people of deep faith. There are these two words, right? We think that progressive and conservative are opposites. Are they opposites? I'm not sure. Because within the conservative, there could be certain progressiveness that I, the progressive, do not have. I may not believe in a certain chant or gospel, or hymn or whatever religion you may belong to. But is it just possible that in the repetition of that chant or gospel, in the utterance of that, there's a certain power that opens the minds in some people? Is it possible that these give that person an ability to be non-divisive in a way that even I can't be? Is it possible? We have to ask these questions because when we don't ask these questions, we push each one of these people away from us and label them as bigots. We almost make sure they run away from us. We make sure that they are caught in the cesspool of anger. I don't blame them. I blame us. I blame you and me. When I say you, I mean people like me for allowing this to happen. So, what I'm trying to say is, right from Independence, I think, there has been a great loss. And that's 70 years of loss in total. It's not today and yesterday, the Constitutional culture was never an umbrella. Because if it was an umbrella, then we would not have had this engaging conversation. Because the Constitution does not belittle any of this.

The Constitution does not disregard any of this. The Constitution is not condescending of people. It does not typecast people as progressive or conservative. The Constitution doesn't call itself liberal. It calls itself equitable and adheres to the ideals equality, fraternity, justice. These are words we give to ourselves, not these divisions within political discourse. What about the way I studied in school? That's a very important part of this conversation. What was my school like? What did I read in my school? People will tell me, there was a time when I went to school, we used to sing these songs where we celebrated every religion. Yes, but what was the conversations that we had around it? Our entire schooling system is discriminative. We have private schools and we have public schools. Everyone listening to this conversation knows who goes to the private school and who goes to the public school. Let's keep that aside. Our education system is casteist. Our education system is discriminative and what we study has nothing to do with being good human beings. How do we expect to create generations of people who are sensitive? How do we expect generations of people to understand cultures or culture? We just use these convenient statements of us being this civilisation that was a melting pot of multiple faiths and cultures. That's not good enough. It has to be felt here in the heart. I'm a person of music. That's what matters to me.

If people lived in the same *mohalla* and had transactions with different communities or different people of different caste groups no. What was their relationship? What did they feel within? If a push came to shove, will one group just get together, gang up and hit the other? Yes, they do. We've seen it happening not just in the last five years but we've seen it happening repeatedly in our history. What have we changed after every one of these incidents?

What have we done? Has there been any healing? And what does healing mean? It means that every once, when something like this happens, we change the way we think, teach and discuss these things. We become more open to these conversations. But, if anything, we have become more closed to these conversations. I'm talking about children, about colleges and schools. Not public intellectuals, not academics, not historians. No, not the books. I'm talking about the classroom. We have not changed that. We still have two pages on the Constitution and a few lines on every religion. I think all this has to change urgently.

Our tone of discourse has to change because it isn't that there is a possibility for the future. It is in these very fundamental changes, the way we embrace, the way we feel, the way we share cultures. What does it really mean to share somebody else's culture? What does it know somebody else's faith? I may be a non-believer, but how do I share in the feeling of faith with another person? I'm not here to give answers to any of this. I don't have answers. I only have doubts. I only have questions. I'm as disturbed as you are. How does one share? How do a believer and a non-believer share culture? How do they do that? What is the preciousness that they share? Is there anything? These are the difficult questions. These are the gaps that we need to address. Because if we don't do that, we probably are just putting 'Band-Aid' again. It is the culmination of decades and decades of letting things just be, turning a blind eye every time something happened beyond that incident. If there is violence, we respond for four months and then we forget about it allowing things to simmer, allowing people to go away from the liberal and open minded conversation, the all encompassing conversation, allowing people to run away because we were intimidating, we are intimidating and has led to where we are today.

I just have a few more things to say before I finish. How does one change what we have today or what we are facing today? How does one change the discourse? How does one think of really a new India? Because I don't really believe that in the larger scheme of things, we really created a new India after 1947. I know people are going to disagree with me, but I'm saying deep inside, yes, there's been progress. Of course, things have changed, and I'll never refute that. A lot of things have changed. Education has happened. People who had no voice have a voice today. But within inside, how do we feel about differences, how do we feel about somebody else? This idea of who's the other? Has that really changed within us? Whether it's caste, whether it's religion or region, has it changed? We still use the term Northeast. We rarely speak about every state. The people of Northeast—of Assam, Manipur, Mizoram, Meghalaya, Nagaland, Arunachal Pradesh—will come and tell you that they are still othered today. How is that happening? Let's go and have a conversation with people who belong to caste groups that are marginalised. They will tell you that even today they feel alone. Lonely. Lonely is a better word. Not alone. Let's go and speak to the Muslims of India, the Christians of India, and ask them how they feel. They will tell you that they feel extremely 'othered', almost told every day. This is a reality because of failing for seven decades. So, what we are seeing today is a compounding of a lacking. We have chosen to address certain things when it is convenient and we have chosen not to address certain things when it was inconvenient. This game of convenience and inconvenience—cultural convenience and cultural inconvenience, religious convenience and religious inconvenience—has allowed us to be facing this monstrosity from the establishment and from the people around. Let's recognise that there is so much anger right now. I can completely disagree with anger, and I do. But the fact is, the anger is true right now. Is the anger entirely generated by external forces? Or are external forces simply triggering something that is deep seated? How does one change the nature of that?

That is our challenge. That deep seated anger. How does one engage with it? We will not be able to speak to people who are in the extremes. But we can speak to a lot of the people who feel it but don't know why they feel it. We can speak to the people who are at the receiving end and wonder why didn't we do anything. We failed them. We have failed the Dalits of India. We have failed the Muslims of India. We have failed the Christians of India. And we have failed talking to people of faith who, within themselves, I will say are good people but have been dragged into the gutter. So this is the challenge we have in front of us. I know I didn't say many happy things and celebrate Indian cultures because I do believe that in just painting that picture, there is no introspection, there's no reflection. I may be wrong with all that I said today and that is not the problem. You can disagree with that. But I feel very deeply about this conversation, because as a musician, I sing songs of faith. I sing songs which are not of faith. I sing songs of society, I sing song of politics, I sing songs of all kinds. They coexist. But I ask my question to myself—how are these songs talking to each other? Am I, as the singer, am able to create a bridge between these songs? Because these songs represent different cultures, different ways of life? Can there be a respectful exchange between these words and these songs and these melodies and these rhythms? And am I, as the voice, giving them the space to breathe and listen to each other? I leave you with the hope that there is sharing between these different ideas of living, of cultures. But let's keep in mind that it's not going to happen automatically. We have to work towards it.

Politics

Modi's Impromptu Foreign Policy

Shashi Tharoor

I am pleased to speak today on the foreign policy of the current ruling dispensation as part of Re-imagining India—a public lecture series organised by India Inclusive to assert an alternative vision of the country countering the bigotry, division and economic failure offered by the ruling party.

When I was Chairman of the Parliament's External Affairs Committee, a position from which I was defenestrated after 5 years (from 2014 to 2019). I always proudly articulated our tradition that our political differences stop at the water's edge—that there isn't any 'Congress foreign policy' or 'Bharatiya Janata Party' (BJP) foreign policy, only Indian foreign policy and Indian national interests. Though the BJP undermined the principle by abandoning the permanent convention under which the committee was always chaired by member of the parliament of the opposition, deciding to replace me with a BJP MP, I still hold to this conviction, even though there are aspects to the Modi government's foreign policy in the last 7 years that are not easy for many to swallow.

The BJP's foreign policy report card has been largely a tale of much activity and few results. Like most Indians, I acknowledge the energy that Narendra Modi has brought to his foreign travels which stand now a hundred trips in the last 7 years to at least 60 countries, even if it means his office still owes an outstanding amount of almost Rs 460 crores to the debt-ridden national carrier Air India as on 2 December 2019.

Mr Modi's desire to introduce himself to the world was entirely understandable, after many years of international ostracism where the only country willing to the grant him a visa seemed to be China. He can be forgiven for over-compensating to some extent. *Asia Times* calculated that Prime Minister Modi was out of his office every 3rd day in his first four years in power, spending 477 out of 1,491 days up till Tuesday, 26 June 2018 in his first term as Prime Minister visiting other countries as well as various Indian States. This is equivalent to a year and three months out of his first four years as Prime Minister. The fifth year, of course, was dominated by his re-election campaign, and since then the 6th and 7th were spent in the COVID-19 pandemic—both of which severally limited his voyages.

The first 4 years were more representative of his travel preferences. Ironically Prime Minister Modi's favourite destination was still China, which he has visited 7 times, but the United States and Germany came close with 5 trips each. His tireless energy is admirable but measurable results are few and far between. It would have been another matter if this extensive travel done by an Indian Prime Minister had actually done the country much good. Our relationship with Pakistan is rocky, China is pushing us around and has taken the lives of Indian jawans, ties with the US are at a low ebb, Nepal mistrusts us and is moving towards China, Maldives refused new visas for Indians for 3 years and so on.

Modi's abundant hugs of world leaders have clearly not borne much fruit. While it is fair to depict the Prime Minister as an energetic salesman abroad for the Government of India, his travel came at expense of domestic priorities, where an over-centralised government's key decisions and appointments were kept pending because of the Prime Minister's unavailability. As India itself under-performed, the credibility of the star salesman himself increasingly came under question. After all, how long can a salesman impress by the sheer-force of oratory and cleverly designed international spectacles, if the package he is selling is largely empty?

Modi has also proved unable to keep his domestic political interests out of his foreign policy. In countries with a substantial Indian population (including the US, UK and Australia but also the UAE, Philippines, Kenya, Singapore, and even Israel) he had special events arranged for him to address the resident Indian community, often in large stadiums like New York's Madison Square Garden or a football stadium in Houston and in London's Wembley. These events were designed to promote the greater glory of Narendra Modi and to denigrate India's achievements before he came to power. On more than one occasion he claimed that Indians were ashamed of their passports till his assumption of office; this line is scarcely calculated to enhance the country's image abroad, even if it serves a narrow political objective back home. Such events reportedly also enhanced the BJP's coffers through generous donations from partisans, attendees and other well-heeled expatriates.

Moreover, worryingly, his visits inevitably sparked a justifiable fear among many observers that the headlines and speeches surrounding his visits were merely 'feel good' bromides that masked growing troubles elsewhere and the serious lack of a cohesive foreign policy blueprint for the country. This is, of course, leaving aside the fact that the '*achhe din*' that were promised to the people of India remain completely out of sight and the phrase has now silently been supplanted by the equally vapid 'New India', an anachronism of dubious substantive content.

Lofty foreign policy pronouncements have helped divert attention from domestic concerns and preserved the image of Modi's India to a large extent at home. I am always amazed by the number of my fellow-citizens who genuinely believe India's stature has gone up on his watch, but even here a feeling of being let down has been mounting for some time. Even the most fervent sympathisers of the prime minister are now beginning to tire of the photo-ops and the 'breaking news' stories of Mr Modi's tireless travels abroad, seemingly with little connection to the needs of the *aam aadmi* at home. And the divisive domestic policies of the government—notably the discriminatory Citizenship Amendment Act, aimed at Muslims, which sparked nationwide protests till the COVID-19 related lockdown shut them down, and the mismanagement of the COVID-19 pandemic itself—have seriously undermined India's credibility.

The government keeps insisting that for the first time the Indians can hold their heads high in the world. The breathtaking falsity of this assertion testifies to the powerful impact of BJP propaganda, assiduously spread through social media outlets like WhatsApp, where repetition alone is enough to secure conviction. But the truth is exactly the opposite: India's stature in the world has never been lower.

It gives me no joy to say this. Even as an Opposition MP, I would like my country to be held in high regard globally, as a thriving democracy and an example to the world of how to manage diversity in a free and open society. Instead, I know that for some time now the world has been troubled by an India that is seen as increasingly bigoted and intolerant, one that is wilfully driving sectarian wedges between its people and being overtaken by an intolerant majoritarianism that has no appeal to the world outside.

Every major newspaper abroad, whether on the right like the *Wall Street Journal* and *Financial Times*, or the left, like *The Guardian* and *The Washington Post*, has published critical editorials about India in recent months and the drumbeat of daily reporting as well as the op-ed columns is relentlessly negative. But the blinkered 'bhakt' sees none of this.

At home, even neutral figures known for their habitual reticence on political matters have expressed alarm. Former Foreign Secretary and NSA Shivshankar Menon said the government's amendment to the Citizenship Act was a 'self-inflicted goal' that has isolated India and resulted in the country being hyphenated with Pakistan as an intolerant state. The divisive policies of the government, he added, has gifted our adversaries 'platforms to attack us'. The global perception of India has changed, 'we have no international support apart from a section of Indian diaspora and some extreme right Members of the European Parliament…and the list of critical voices in the international community is also pretty long.'

Referring to Bangladesh Home Minister Asaduzzaman Khan's comment on India's troubles in 2019—'let them fight amongst themselves'—Menon added, 'If this is how our friends feel, think of how happy this will make our adversaries'. Several world leaders, including French President Emmanuel Macron, German Chancellor Angela Merkel, the visiting Norwegian King, and chiefs of UN bodies on human rights and refugees, were critical of the government's moves on the CAA and Kashmir. Thanks to the government's dramatic and undemocratic suspension of its autonomy and statehood, Kashmir has been discussed in the UN Security Council again after 40 years.

For a government driven by (and drawing political capital from) its lavishly funded publicity machine, this is becoming a problem. India, as I have said often, needs to strike a balance between its hard power and soft power: it is not the country with the bigger army that wins but that which tells the better story. At the moment, the story Mr Modi and his colleagues in government are pitching to the world looks less and less convincing with every passing month. If foreign policy were merely a question of making fine speeches, then the prime minister would score top marks. But substance must follow grandiloquent oratory. Unfortunately for Mr Modi, he has very little substance to show for his efforts abroad, and only a shipload more of promises to add to the titanic stock already piled high at home.

Hindutva ideologues have tried to construct a distinctive 'Modi doctrine' in foreign policy. A book of that name, published under the auspices of the RSS-affiliated Dr Syama Prasad Mookerjee Research Foundation, even lays out its five principal features: 'Samman—dignity and honour; Samvad—greater engagement and dialogue; Samriddhi—shared prosperity; Suraksha—regional and global security; and Sanskriti evam Sabhyata—cultural and civilizational linkages.' But aside from the Sanskrit terms, it is difficult to see how these five ideas differ from the policy principles of previous Indian governments. Modi's current Foreign Minister, who had been Foreign Secretary for three years (2015-18), S Jaishankar, the senior civil servant in the Ministry of External Affairs, famously suggested that India, earlier content with being a 'balancing power', was now seeking, under Narendra Modi, to be a 'leading power'. But how precisely the Modi government has set about achieving this remains a mystery. A grandiloquent speech by RSS chief Mohan Bhagwat, head of the organisation of which Modi has been a lifetime *pracharak*, declaring that India was on its way to becoming a vishwa guru (teacher of the world), embarrassingly summed up both the pretensions and the embarrassment of India's global self-projection. We have a government that believes its own press releases even when those they are directed at ignore them.

What the world thinks matters more to us than ever before. Not least because we are far more dependent on external trade and investment than we ever were. But foreign investment is an act of trust and faith in the future which is fast eroding. Our credit ratings have declined; seven countries have issued travel warnings about India. And the world increasingly sees us as an intolerant, narrow-minded nation, in open violation of our international commitments. For years India was seen as an example or a model for countries in the developing world. Now the ruling party's sectarian, divisive actions driven by narrow party-political goals, have severely dented that image.

I too was proud to hold my head high as an Indian abroad. Today I am mortified when foreigners ask me to explain what's going on, what's happening to India in the last few years. The sad answer is that we have ceased to be an India that the world admired.

One concrete achievement by Prime Minister Modi's foreign policy appears to be that of getting the United Nations to adopt International Yoga Day, since it has meant people around the world following an Indian practice in a highly visible way that enhances our global image, with yoga events taking place at prominent locations around the world (though the manner in which the government subsequently pursued the Guinness Book of World Records over the issue was, to put it mildly, unseemly). That, alas, is the extent of the positive side of the ledger, where the PM's efforts have borne tangible results. For the rest, the report card is decidedly troubling.

India's foreign policy appears to many observers to be created impromptu, on the hoof, as it were, in the course of the prime minister's peripatetic travels. Key discussions which should have taken place in the preparation of these visits seem to follow the prime minister's pronouncements, rather than precede and justify them. The announcements, usually of investments to come, have largely failed to materialise. And stated goals, such as those accompanying the impressive India-African Summit in New Delhi or the bold promises of $100 billion in Chinese investments during Xi Jinping's visit in September 2014, do not seem to be accompanied by the investment of adequate resources to fulfil them or coordination with various government agencies to achieve their announced goals. The summit showcased this government's tendency to see such occasions as events to be well managed, rather than part of a strategy requiring meticulous implementation. And the $100 billion was eventually watered down to $30 billion, served with an embarrassing side order of incursions by the PLA, audaciously while Xi was still on Indian soil. Very little of even that $30 billion has actually arrived in India, and now after tragedy in Galwan in 2020 summer, even what was coming has been halted.

Indeed, in the first Modi term, the External Affairs Ministry did not appear to be involved in much serious follow-up work to the PM's tours. Fundamental decisions were taken in the PMO, if not by the prime minister himself, along with his national security adviser. And while the late external affairs minister, Sushma Swaraj, was herself a respected and widely-liked politician, her role in the formulation of foreign policy appeared to be so tightly circumscribed that diplomats in Delhi referred to her, with a somewhat disparaging smile, as the minister for consular affairs. Her time was spent largely on Twitter, replying to voters' complaints about her ministry's services, helping Indians who had lost their passports abroad and Pakistanis needing heart surgery in India—not to mention the largely pointless effort to splurge taxpayers' money to secure Hindi as an official language at the United Nations. Meanwhile, the ministry had to swallow the embarrassment of seeing 'Yoga and Indian Culture Acharyas' (well-versed in Sanskrit, yoga and the Hindu scriptures) appointed with diplomatic status at Indian Embassies to promote Hindu culture abroad, even as its core diplomatic staff languishes at levels comparable to New Zealand and Singapore, countries of considerably smaller population and modest global aspiration. The gap between the aspirations Mr Modi loves to speak of and the capacity of the Ministry of External Affairs to fulfil them has never been more glaring.

Where has Mr Modi's India been found wanting in the process? The red ink on the Prime Minister's report card begins with our neighbourhood, which is where any government must act with greater caution and sensitivity to balance our national interest with regional circumstances beyond our control.

Since Mr Modi's swearing in—a pageant of sorts that saw the premiers of Pakistan, Nepal, Sri Lanka and Afghanistan in attendance and which was lauded as the grand inauguration of a new chapter in our international relations—India's ties with Pakistan have witnessed more ups and downs than a child's yo-yo. The prime minister—a man who systematically obstructed the UPA government's peacemaking efforts with Pakistan and whose campaign speeches thrived on demonising that country—had excoriated the Congress for 'serving chicken biryani' to a Pakistani visitor. Now he was exchanging shawls and saris with his Islamabad counterpart, along with sentimental letters to each other's mothers.

I mischievously tweeted my hope that chicken biryani must be on the Prime Minister's dinner menu for his Pakistani guest, but I believe it wasn't.

By inviting Nawaz Sharif to Delhi when he took office in 2014, Mr Modi was believed to have turned a historic page and opened a new era of bilateral relations. But less than two months had passed before both countries were exchanging artillery fire across the still-sensitive border. Talks between our respective foreign secretaries were called off when the Pakistanis proposed meeting Indian Kashmiri separatist leaders on their proposed visit—something our visitors had always done and to which earlier governments had responded with confident official indifference. In November of the same year, at the SAARC summit in Nepal, Mr Modi pointedly stared at a brochure to ignore his Pakistani counterpart as he walked past, though it was later revealed that the two leaders had met privately in a hotel suite belonging to an Indian businessman. The pattern repeated itself in December 2015, when Mr Modi made an impromptu visit to Lahore to attend a celebration at Mr Sharif's home; a week later relations turned frosty again after seven Indians were killed by Pakistani militants at the Pathankot Air Force Base, later followed by an equally condemnable attack on the Indian army at Uri in September 2016 and at Nagrota the month after. In retribution, the Indian army conducted a series of 'surgical strikes', lightning precision attacks, on terrorist camps operating out of Pakistani soil. While the nation rightfully applauded the swift response of our armed forces, the present government appeared to be more preoccupied with spinning the strike as the first of its kind—a testament to the supposed iron mind of their prime minister. This was blatantly untrue: it is now well known that similar strikes have been ordered in the past but not publicised. Then came, on the eve of the 2019 General Elections, a terrorist attack in Pulwama, Kashmir, to which India retaliated with a bombing of Balakot, Pakistan, which was described as having eliminated a terrorist training camp, though much of the international media echoed Pakistan's contention that only a few trees on a deserted hillside were hit. Worse, the entire approach reflects the lack of a cohesive policy framework when it comes to negotiating the relationship with our most turbulent neighbour.

India–Pakistan relations have swung back and forth, as though they are determined more by the unpredictable moods of our leadership than on a coherent foreign policy and vision for peace, let alone a practical roadmap. One day the government declares its 'red lines' and twice calls off talks with Pakistan because its representatives met with the Kashmiri-separatist Hurriyat; the next day the red lines don't matter. One day the ruling party avers that talks and terror don't go together and that Pakistan cannot be rewarded with a visit till it makes progress on punishing the perpetrators of 26/11; the next day the PM is winging impulsively to Lahore, sending India's surprised high commissioner scurrying to the airport to receive his boss. This is foreign policy by whim, not by design.

So too with Nepal—where New Delhi's de facto blockade choked the nation's economy, cut off its oil supplies, created genuine hardship and provoked a groundswell of hostility among ordinary Nepalis. This, and the behaviour that accompanied the episode, was a blunder of such Himalayan proportions that the only country on earth whose relationship with us has been fraternal enough for us to maintain open borders with it, now shows every sign of turning towards China instead. Telling then, of the current strain in relations, is the fact that once Prime Minister K P Sharma Oli was sworn into office for the second time in 2018, the first leader to visit his country was his Pakistani counterpart Shahid Khaqan Abbasi. Now an unseemly border dispute has inflamed tensions in 2020.

One astute observer told me privately that 'PMO took its eyes off the ball on Nepal'. But when decision-making has been so centralised in the Modi regime that every ministry has to send its important files to the PMO for clearance, how many balls can Mr Modi and his beleaguered minions keep their eyes on?

India's mess in Nepal adds to the growing sense of disquiet amongst students of Indian foreign policy about the Modi government's management of relations on the subcontinent. A combination of arrogance and ineptitude is all too often visible. where subtlety and proactive diplomacy could have delivered the desired results. A raid into Myanmar in hot pursuit of terrorist sanctuaries had six precedents under the UPA, but each had been shrouded in a discreet silence; the Modi government chose to announce their one raid with such bellicose rhetoric that it embarrassed Myanmar, the violation of whose sovereignty New Delhi was trumpeting.

Relations with our neighbours—Pakistan, Nepal and until a recent change of government, the Maldives—are worse than they have ever been. The Modi government's fecklessness has caused negative consequences for private Indian interests too. The Maldives not only cancelled projects involving Indian companies, but turned away Indian applications for employment visas, leading resorts to advertise posts open to any nationalities but 'Indians need not apply'. Meanwhile China was signing contracts previously offered to Indians, and Chinese and Pakistani warships were calling on Maldivian ports. Good relations have now been restored, but that they ever plunged to such depths remains a matter of serious concern.

On the wider global stage, the list of failures is dizzyingly high. The US, for all of PM Modi's visits, played fast and loose in 2018-19 with the so-called '2+2' (where the foreign and defence ministers of both countries meet) dialogue with India being postponed twice and tensions over trade tariffs reaching an all-time high, with each country slapping tariffs on the other's products. The US sent its Indian-origin ambassador to the UN, Nikki Haley, to instruct the Modi government to curb its links with Iran. As India cut back, China stepped into the breach with Iran, jeopardising its geopolitical interests on Pakistan's western flank. At the same time the Modi government's unctuous currying of favour with the US has led to a precipitous decline in relations with Russia, with the much-touted joint fifth-generation aircraft project being abandoned. Even on the recent Afghanistan crisis, Russia had taken a neutral stand on India's interests there, rather than a sympathetic one. Within the US itself, the bipartisan consensus on strong India-US relations that used to exist for the last 25 years, irrespective of which governments were in power in Delhi or Washington, has been broken. All the significant Democratic presidential candidates in the 2020 elections spoke out about their concerns, while the 'Howdy Modi' administration is closely identified with President Trump ('Abki Baar Trump Sarkar', in our PM's words). Hearings have been held in the US Congress, negative language on Kashmir has been inserted into the annual Foreign Appropriations Act for 2020, and a resolution critical of India gained more co-sponsors than expected.

The picture is not much better elsewhere. European relations are adrift and Britain remains bemused by its dealing with our prime minister. Despite a few announcements of aid and trade made during Mr Modi's visit to Africa for the BRICS summit in July 2018, our engagement with the continent has proved to be a sorry tale of high-level neglect.

China's is a particularly a disappointing story. Indeed, the most glaring embarrassment in our recent foreign policy has been the way Modi's government has handled India's relationship with China, starting with the fiasco of President Xi's over-hyped visit in 2014 and culminating in the complete mismanagement of the military stand-off between the two countries in Doklam, which the government claimed had been resolved in a triumph for Indian diplomacy in August 2017. The PR exercise that Modi Inc managed to spin from that event was undone a few months later when consistent reports and publicly available satellite imagery all pointed to the fact that, despite Indian claims of 'victory', the Chinese had consolidated their presence on the Himalayan plateau that directly overlooks India's strategic Siliguri corridor, and had been doing so for some time. Worse, the ongoing Chinese encroachments across the Line of Actual Control in a number of locations, and the deaths of 20 Indian soldiers in a clash in the Galwan Valley in June 2020, followed by the stubborn refusal of the Chinese to return to the status quo ante in the area, showed how much India had failed to safeguard its own interests in the bilateral relationship.

But the inconsistency in this government's foreign policy style and narrative is not new. In the lead-up to and during his election campaign in 2014, Narendra Modi and the BJP had constantly berated the Government of India for being unable to do anything about frequent Chinese incursions across the disputed frontier. Two years later, the same Mr Modi not only embarked on a stream of effusive meetings with both the Chinese president (with whom he shared much publicised bonhomie on several occasions, meeting him 18 times in six years), but also invited China to help modernise the

Indian railways and removed government restrictions on Chinese investment in sensitive sectors like ports and telecoms. As to the border incursions, the BJP government echoed the very line it had denounced when the Congress government uttered it—that since the two countries have differing perceptions of where the border lies, each patrols in areas the other considers to be theirs. What was excoriated by Mr Modi as pusillanimity and appeasement in the Congress have now, overnight, become wisdom and statesmanship in the BJP.

Meanwhile, China has shown no inclination to make progress on the intractable border dispute between the two countries. It has extended overt protection to Pakistan after the Modi government's belligerent PR offensive on the 'strategic strikes'; it has displaced India in the Maldives; thwarted an Indian deal to set up a naval base in the Seychelles; and through the China–Pakistan Economic Corridor, a $62 billion project, it has outflanked India by creating a strategic transportation link between the Pakistani port of Gwadar—which China, to all intents and purposes, controls and runs—western to its own Western provinces, partly through territory that India claims. And now China is talking to the Taliban Government in Afghanistan, where it is hoping to explore minerals and integrate Afghanistan and Pakistan into its own CPEC. I must say India has much to worry about.

While the Modi government desperately tries to cover up its shortcomings by claiming nothing has gone wrong (the Prime Minister has even said no territory has been taken), China's actions suggest an intention to undertake minor military incursions in order to inflict small-scale military setbacks on India, take a few square kilometres of territory for local tactical purposes, and then declare peace. Mutual disengagements will be announced, both sides will claim the crisis is over, but it will end with the Chinese in a better position on the ground than before it began. With several such episodes a year, none of which usually get out of hand, China will consolidate the LAC where it wants it, so that an eventual border settlement that takes these new realities into account will be in its favour. That is the long-term plan: Beijing keeps saying the border should be left to future generations to settle, knowing full well that each passing year increases China's relative economic, military and geopolitical strength vis-à-vis India. In the meantime, border incidents keep the Indians off balance and demonstrate to the world that India is not capable of challenging China, let alone offering security to other nations. It is difficult not to see China policy as anything but a major failure of the Modi government.

There have of course been some foreign policy successes, but these have almost entirely been in areas where Mr Modi and his party chose to follow the path already laid by successive previous governments without upsetting the delicate balance upon which these relationships rested. One of the prime minister's greatest achievements is that he has reversed the BJP's formal opposition in Parliament to the Indo–US Nuclear Deal and to the seminal land boundary agreement with Bangladesh—both of which were UPA initiatives and both of which were wise policy reversals by the NDA government of the positions the BJP had taken in opposition. In a continuation of UPA policy and as a reflection of the country's image as a responsible nuclear power, India was subsequently admitted to three global missile-nuclear technology groupings.

In the 2014 and 2019 election campaigns, Narendra Modi had breathed fire and brimstone about Bangladesh, accusing it of sending millions of illegal immigrants—'termites', as his Home Minister indelicately dubbed them—into India and promising that the moment he won the election, they would all have to 'pack their bags' and leave India for home. Bangladeshi officials had publicly and privately expressed their disquiet that any attempt to do this could be deeply destabilising for their politically fragile state. Within weeks of his 2014 victory, however, Modi's foreign minister was all smiles on her first official visit abroad—to Bangladesh. Illegal immigration wasn't even mentioned in Dhaka. The Land Boundary Agreement with Bangladesh concluded by Prime Minister Manmohan Singh, which Indian diplomats had considered vital to removing bilateral irritants, had never been implemented because UPA couldn't win the BJP's support in Parliament to ratify the territorial swaps required. But now the Modi government is the biggest votary of the Land Boundary Agreement, which the Opposition co-operated fully in ratifying.

However, the BJP government in Assam has unwisely reopened the issue of deportations, and disquiet is mounting in our friendly neighbour as the National Register of Citizens in Assam identified individuals to be 'foreigners' who are potentially deportees. There is, however, no deportation agreement in place between India and Bangladesh. The heated debates over the Citizenship Amendment Bill, including the Indian Home Minister's indelicate description of Bangladeshis as 'termites', further vitiated the atmosphere, leading to an unprecedented situation in which the Indian High Commissioner was unable to call on the Bangladeshi President for months despite repeated unsuccessful attempts.

The BJP had been virulently critical of the Indo–US nuclear deal, Manmohan Singh's signature foreign policy triumph. They had even supported a no-confidence motion against the UPA government on the issue of the deal. Yet, in a quiet and under-reported move, the Modi government wisely ratified the India-specific Additional Protocol, a UPA undertaking to grant greater access to India's civilian nuclear sites to the UN's International Atomic Energy Agency.

The one brief success of recent Indian foreign policy—its 'vaccine diplomacy', which sent Indian-manufactured vaccines in the first months of 2021 to 90 foreign countries—turned to ashes when the second wave of the COVID-19 pandemic caught the government napping. As the infection rate and death toll in India mounted, the government could not explain why more vaccines had been dispatched abroad than injected in India. It then slapped an export ban on India's vaccines, destroying not only the government's credibility but exposing the country's leading vaccine manufacturer, the Serum Institute of India, to punitive action for failing to fulfil its contractual obligations to supply vaccines that had already been paid for.

On the rather meagre credit side of the ledger, I would also say this government's Africa policy has been a qualified success, although a lot more could have been done and the level of inattention to the continent remains disappointing. Here again, though, what PM Modi is doing, more often than not, is building on the foundations laid by the UPA government.

After all, where you stand on foreign policy, it is clear, depends on where you sit. Your stand is different when you're sitting in South Block and not in Gandhinagar.

The cerebral American politician, New York Governor Mario Cuomo, once memorably observed that you campaign in poetry, but govern in prose. Hard reality, he suggested, replaces the flights of policy fantasy that afflict those without power. The video clips of Narendra Modi, the Opposition leader, berating the UPA government's foreign policies have come to haunt Narendra Modi, the Prime Minister. While his old poetry was savagely acerbic, the nation has discovered that, on the subject of foreign policy, his prose has dried up.

Contemporary India: Issues & Challenges

D Raja

Respected comrades and friends,

The battle to retain the idea of India has become very intense today. A few days back, I addressed a campaign that strives to reclaim India, but now, the present campaign is for reimagining India. What is this India, we want to reimagine? I was the General Secretary of All India Youth Federation from 1985-1990, I worked from Delhi, the national capital, travelling all over the country. During that period, we organised long marches from Kanyakumari to Delhi, from Manipur to Delhi, from Hussainiwala to Delhi, from Kashmir to Delhi. The slogan of those marches was, 'Save India and Change India'. How to change, how to save—were the questions before us. When we say save India, from whom do we want to save it? How to change India for a better future? We tried our best to mobilise the young generation, the youth and students and people at large on this clarion call of 'Save India Change India'.

That was the time, the neo-liberal economic policies were introduced and implemented by the government. That was the time, the question on reservation became very sharp, the Mandal Commission Report was taken up for debate across the country and by the government for implementation. That was the time, when communal fascist forces, the Hindutva forces intensified their campaign on what was popularly known as the *Mandir*. It was the time, people described as a period of struggle between *Mandal* and *Kamandal*. So, our Youth Federation organised the 'Save India Change India' campaign. This is an issue which was addressed by the freedom fighters, in the post-independent India, started from

B R Ambedkar, Jawaharlal Nehru and many communists, they tried to imagine how India should be.

During the debates in the Constituent Assembly, the Hindutva forces pressurised Ambedkar to declare India a Hindurashtra. Ambedkar, in his vision, empathically rejected the theocratic idea of India. Ambedkar made it clear that if India has to emerge as an independent nation, then it should emerge as democratic republic. Ambedkar pointed out, if at all the Hindurashtra should become a reality, that will be the biggest disaster for India. Then Ambedkar made it clear in the post-independent India, what should be the character of the state. The Constitution makes it clear that the Indian State should be secular. It should be above all religions thus maintaining harmony among all sections of the people. Indian State should be a welfare state and ensure all means of livelihood to all its citizens. For this, the state should see that wealth and means of production are not concentrated in the hands of a few people and that the general people have access to education, employment, housing, and above all, the right to live with dignity. This is how Ambedkar defined what the Indian State should be.

But today, the battle between the two visions has become very intensive. One vision, presented by the BJP-RSS (Bharatiya Janata Party-Rashtriya Swayamsevak Sangh) combine, is trying to hijack the 'thinking' of the people. Now, it is a big irony in history, the RSS was formed in the year 1925, that was also the year the Communist Party of India was formed. The Communist Party of India has made supreme sacrifices for winning Independence from the British Raj. And the RSS had no role at all in the freedom movement. Today the RSS and the BJP, which is the political wing of the RSS, have come to power. Ideologically, RSS is a sectarian, divisive, communal, and fascist organisation. And the BJP government acts on the basis of this ideology, what do they say, what is this ideology, we should try to understand that the RSS tries to impose Hindutva agenda, thereby to impose a monolithic, illiberal, medieval, socio-political order on the people of our country.

The other vision is that India should remain a secular, democratic republic and the diversity of the country should be recognised and celebrated. India has got a number of languages—ancient and modern both—as well as a rich cultural grounding. Different parts of this huge country come with diverse elements of history and culture and all of it should be respected.

Today, the struggle is between these two visions—to uphold and safeguard the secular, democratic, and the republican vision of India and to establish Hindutva based theocratic, monolithic India, which is dictatorial, authoritarian India. As far as the Communist Party of India is concerned, we are in the midst of these ideological, political struggles and electoral struggles. We have been fighting; in fact, we have been trying to unite all secular democratic forces in this struggle against the communal fascists.

Look at the present government headed by the BJP-RSS; on one side, they impose the Hindutva agenda in every sphere of our social life. They are changing the character of education and all other social policies in our country. That is why our struggle has become intensive. Today, the RSS-BJP combine is trying to re-define India on the basis of the Hindutva ideology. They are trying to subvert the Indian Constitution, which is a republican Constitution. They want to build a theocratic, authoritarian rule. They want to carry forward India as they please. The present government headed by Narendra Modi is acting with such a determination and commitment to serve the interest of the international finance capital, and corporate crony capitalists. They encourage all communal fascist movements in our country. What we witness today is crony capitalism and authoritarian fascism. This vision of India presented by the RSS-BJP combine should be rejected emphatically, it is not a vision at all.

We should present our alternative vision of India. India should be a democracy. People should have access to education, employment, and housing and should feel that they live in a free country and lead a life with dignity. People should have access to the wealth of their nation.

Today, India is in the grip of three fundamental challenges. First is caste discrimination or social discrimination. Second, class exploitation, the perpetuation of looting the surplus values created by the toiling masses, the working people. Third, patriarchy. I think the time has come that the progressive, democratic, and revolutionary forces must take up these issues.

In India, caste is one of the fundamental issues. It is not only the superstructure but it has also formed the base of the structure. B R Ambedkar said that wherever you go, the monster of caste will follow along. You may talk of political reform, economic reform, but unless you kill that monster, there will be no progress and no change. We cannot talk of social justice when caste based social discrimination still exists. The Constitution very clearly says '*We, the People of India*'. It does not say we the Hindus, we the Brahmins, we the Muslims or we the Shudras.

The Constitution teaches us to strive for justice—social, political, and economic. How to establish this justice? We keep talking about revolution—*Inquilab Zindabad*—what is *Inquilab* in India? What is revolution in India? We have to fight against social discrimination and caste discrimination, we have to fight against economic exploitation, we have to intensify class struggle and also fight against patriarchy. Then only we can accomplish revolution and mobilise people. These three issues must be addressed by all revolutionary and secular forces. We have to fight against caste discrimination, social injustice, economic exploitation; liberating the working people from the loot of surplus labour, and surplus value, and we have to fight against patriarchy. Unless we do all these, we cannot have the India that we are trying to imagine.

I am from Thiruvallur in Tamil Nadu and there, it is said '*pirapokkum ella uyirkkum*'—birth is the same for all living creature, how come human beings are divided in the name of caste, religion, or even class? Why should these divisions even exist? These divisions should be removed. If at all these things happen, we cannot have the India we are trying to imagine—a prosperous, happy country where people have love and compassion for each other.

When I say, 'Save India', I mean save India from these communal fascist forces, from crony capitalist corporate houses who are looting the country.

Friends and comrades, when we reimagine India, we should also understand that in our struggle, we should find Marx-Ambedkar coming closer; we find communists—Ayyankali, Sri Narayan Guru, and EV Ramaswami Periyar in Tamil Nadu, all these great fighters come together ideologically. It has become necessary that communists, Marxist, Ambedkarites must come together. Communists, Marxist, Periyarists must come together. Ideologically, we should build a strong united fight against the Hindutva ideology, the fascist ideology of the RSS-BJP.

We all should strive for protecting the country's wealth, to protect the public sector, fighting against privatisation, foreign capital, direct investment and international finance capital. In the given situation we should fight for the rights of women in all walks of life and that will pave the ground for a new India, which we all imagine.

As a communist, I think India will emerge as socialist India. When we talk of socialism that will be with Indian characteristics, we cannot think of other models. India will have its own road to socialism. India will have its own path to socialism. Marxism should be applied to the local conditions, concrete conditions of our country. What are those concrete conditions? To get rid of caste, class and patriarchy. How to change this and how to take the country forward towards socialism? Socialism with Indian characteristics must be our understanding. Here, the communists have a special role, to work with other secular and democratic forces to unite them and take them along in their common struggle against communal fascists and the BJP-RSS. That will be the ground for our imagining or reimagining a new India with a new vision.

Threats to Our Republic: The Need to Reclaim It

Prashant Bhushan

Rethinking about the idea of India can happen at two levels. At one level, we could talk about the kind of India would we like to have. What should be the nature of its people? What should be the state of the environment? What should be the kind of education that is given to our citizens? What should be the nature of healthcare? What should be the type of our democracy itself? What should be the material needs of people in our country and our society? At the other level, we can ask what kind of laws, institutions and systems need to be put in place to imagine and to achieve the kind of India that we want.

First, we must understand that our Constitution provides us with a fairly good model of visualising a kind of India that our Constitution makers had imagined. So, they imagined a democratic and pluralistic society; a society which would be driven by scientific temper, where people would have various Fundamental Rights and a society where institutions such as the Election Commission, Comptroller and Auditor General, a free judiciary, media, etc, would be put in place to help us achieve those ends. But even though the Constitution makers did a very good job of putting in place the kinds of systems and institutions that were needed, I think we still fall short of what needs to be done.

To reduce the short falls, we first need to imagine a society, which is diverse, not just in terms of religion, but also ethnicity and language. Just as biodiversity is an asset of environment, human diversity of every kind is also a great asset for society. Secondly, while the Constitution imagined and spoke about the need to inculcate scientific temper, it did not speak so much about critical thinking or about developing an understanding of empathy towards other people, other beings, and to the environment in general. So, one of the things that we would like to imagine further in our society would be that education should be driven with the objective of creating people who have a highly developed sense of critical thinking, where they are able to question everything and arrive at their own conclusions on the basis of reasoning, discussions, thinking etc through the cultivation of scientific temper. Beyond that, we need a kind of education that will inculcate in them a sense of empathy towards their fellow beings.

If we focus education on these two broad objectives, that is, critical thinking and scientific temper on one hand and empathy on the other, then we would have created human beings who not only love and live in harmony with each other and also nature, but are also empowered, because of the highly developed sense of critical thinking.

So far as material needs are concerned, our Constitution does not say much except that we must strive to reduce economic inequality amongst people. However, it does not quite talk about the need for everybody to have a dignified job which, in my opinion, should be a Fundamental Right. Of course, the Supreme Court, while interpreting Article 21, the Right to Life and Liberty, said that it does not mean the Right to Animal Life or Liberty, it means the Right to lead a dignified life and the cardinal requirement of it is to have a dignified job or work. The Constitution doesn't talk much about Health Care either, but it is absolutely necessary to provide to all free and reasonable basic healthcare in order to achieve the goal of ensuring a dignified life. Health care is unfortunately being understood in terms of allopathic medicines and institutions which are largely driven by profit driven. We need to get out of this mentality and develop healthcare systems which are holistic in nature. There are many things in our medicines—Ayurved, Naturopathy, etc, which are effective and need to be part of the whole healthcare—medical curriculum, education, and understanding.

The Constitution imagines that we would be a Democracy, but it does not spell out in clear terms the kind of Democracy it wants India to be. Probably the architects of the Constitution had felt that we need to be a Representative Democracy. But now, it is well known and well understood that there are many ways of direct democracy which have been practised and have been put in place in many other countries of the world. We too can move on similar lines. For example, we can have initiatives and referendums by which people can directly say what is the kind of law or system that they want to put in place and if sufficient number of people sign in that initiative, then a referendum can be held to decide whether a majority of the people want that or not. There are other ways of achieving a more participatory democracy, first is of course the decentralisation of power so that we can have more town hall meetings, 'Gram Sabhas', etc, in which decisions can be taken by the physical presence of all the stake holders of that community.

We need to move from Representative Democracy to Participatory Democracy, because, within Representative Democracy we have adopted, unfortunately, the 'first past the post system' at two levels. That is, when we elect our representatives, we elect only one person who gets the maximum votes, even if s/he gets only 25% of the votes, so long as others have got less than him. So, even if the other candidates, put together, get 75% of the votes, the one who gets 25% of the votes provided it is the highest vote percentage, becomes the sole representative. Thereafter, when we elect a Government, the Party or the Coalition, which has a majority in the Assembly or Parliament gets to form the whole Government, with the opposition counting as nothing, even if they have 49% of the seats.

This 'first past the post' at two levels has created a system in which those parties or candidates, who enjoy great visibility, get an enormous privilege of being elected. They don't necessarily vote for the person or the party they consider the best, if they feel that the candidate or party has virtually no chance of getting elected. So, they vote for the least bad among those candidates that they feel has some chance of getting elected. The judgement is made on the basis of visibility of the candidates and we know that visibility is a product of money. So, this 'first past the post system' has privileged the use of and given a huge advantage of those candidates and parties who have a lot of money. Therefore, we need to change the system and put into order other system like proportional representation which is there in many countries. Now, in order to achieve all these objectives, we need people of a certain kind whose mindset is directed towards achieving these objectives.

The most important institution in a society and in our country is the Judiciary. We need a Judiciary not merely to decide disputes but to enforce Fundamental Rights, to ensure that the Executive and the Legislature function within the bounds of their respective jurisdiction and do their jobs. We need a Judiciary which is totally independent of the government. To ensure that the Judiciary is unbiased, its independence is imperative. One way of doing that is to prevent the judges from getting post-retirement jobs in which the government has any say whatsoever. 'Master of Roster' is a system where the Chief Justice alone decides which case will be heard by which bench. Therefore, if the government has control over Judiciary, it will be able to control the entire court procedures because all sensitive cases, all important cases from the government's point of view can be listed before judges of their choice. The power of deciding which case will be listed before which bench should not be exercised only by the Chief Justice but by a collegium of minimum of five senior judges. Thereafter, we need to improve the system of selecting judges. Earlier, the government used to select judges; now these senior judges of the Supreme Court are supposed to select judges. Even this system has many flaws, one of which is the lack of transparency. The other is that there are no criteria which is fixed for selecting judges.

Thus, we need a full-time body which is completely independent of the government and it should be tasked with the job of selecting judges, especially of the higher judiciary. Then of course, we need to increase the number of courts so that justice is dispensed quickly and for that we need to effectuate the 'Gram Nayalayas', which were envisaged to be the first lowest courts at the block levels, where at least ordinary disputes could be decided by following an informal procedure, without having to engage lawyers, which most people cannot afford in our country.

One more reform that we need is to have Judicial Accountability. There should be a Judicial Accountability Commission or a Judicial Complaints Commission—a very high-level body which should also be completely independent of the government as well as of the Judiciary so that it can hold the judges to account, entertain complaints against judges and take action against judges who are errant or corrupt in any particular way.

Media is another important institution which has collapsed in this country and is now completely subservient to government control by such methods as inducements, giving government advertisement to its favoured people in the media, etc. Thereafter, also using Investigative Agencies punitively in order to harass, intimidate and penalise those sections of the media that don't fall in line. So, firstly, we need to have an independent body which can ensure that government advertisements are not unfairly given. Secondly, regulatory institutions like a Media Council should be empowered to ensure that the media is not harassed by investigating agencies under the control of the government. Thirdly, we need to prevent large corporations from coming to control sections of the media. We need some kind of an Anti-Trust Body to look into media monopolies and prevent the same. And fourthly, we need to gain this kind of independent media council which could take actions against the misconduct by media because that pose a serious problem today. Then there are all these investigative agencies like the Central Bureau of Investigation (CBI), the Enforcement Directorate (ED), the National Investigation Agency (NIA), various police agencies, the Lokpal, etc, which need to be made completely independent of the government. There was a big Lokpal Movement after which the Lokpal Law was brought in. But unfortunately, it has not been able to significantly contribute. So, for selecting all the heads and all the important people in all these investigative agencies we need to have a selection committee which is completely independent of the government. The same problem is happening with the Election Commission also, another important institution, which is supposed to regulate free and fair elections. Election Commission members too are appointed by the government. The selection of the Comptroller and Auditor General, is still left under the control of the government.

The Supreme Court had issued various directions about Police Reforms in the Prakash Singh case in 2006.[1] There was a slew of reforms which had been directed but unfortunately even 15 years down the line, that judgment has still not been implemented. We need to ensure that judgment gets implemented without undue delays. Though a few reforms have been introduced, for example, the Right to Information Act, a lot more needs to be done. There is an utmost need for strengthening the system of selection and appointment in these institutions so that transparency is maintained always. People must always be made aware of the selection process—the method by which selections are done, whether everybody has a fair chance to apply or if the names of the shortlisted persons are being put out in the public domain, etc.

In this regard, we might mention this incident that occurred sometime back. Justice Arun Mishra's selection as the Chairman of the National Human Rights Commission (2021) has attracted widespread controversy. Justice Arun Mishra, during his tenure in the Supreme Court, never gave any significant judgment against the government; on the contrary, it is said that he always sided with the government on all important issues, virtually in every important adjudication. Contrary to all rules, Justice Mishra was allowed, as a special case, to overstay in his official bungalow for nine months after his retirement from the Supreme Court. While discharging his duties as the head of the National Human Rights Commission, people are, therefore, sceptical as to the extent Justice Mishra could be critical about the government orders/deeds.

So, there are a large number of institutions which still need to be reformed; some of the reforms which had been done, for example, a very good, Right to Information Act (2005) was brought and there was supposed to be independent information commissioners who were supposed to enforce that act, but today what we see is that information commissioners are not being appointed, those posts are being left vacant or even when they are filled in, the people who are ex-bureaucrats and close to the ruling political parties are being appointed.

So in all these cases we see the need for strengthening the system of selection and appointment of people who man these institutions. Firstly, there must be much greater transparency in the system so that people can see how the persons are selected, what is the method by which people are being appointed, that everybody has a fair chance to apply etc, the shortlisted persons' names are being put out in the public domain when the appointments are finally made, so that people who know anything about them can send their comments about them; this we must see across the board in all the regulatory institutions—these kind of reforms need to be made. So, these are the changes that we require in all these institutions to ensure that these institutions function for the purpose for which they were designed, namely to protect Fundamental Rights, to protect Democracy and to protect other values which are enshrined in the Constitution.

NOTE

1 Prakash Singh vs Union of India; Prakash Singh, the former DGP of Uttar Pradessh and Assam Police filed a PIL in the Supreme Court post retirement, in 1996, seeking police reforms. In a landmark judgment, the Supreme Court, in September 2006, had directed all the states and union territories to bring in a series of measures that were to be undertaken by the governments.

Erosion of the Constitutional Rights, and a Plan for Retrieval

Sukumar Muralidharan

On the eve of India's independence, a British civil servant, Malcolm Darling set off on horseback across the country. His intention was to speak to the people of India and to gather their range of opinions on what freedom meant. He encountered a bewildering array of opinions. For some, freedom meant freedom from the landlord from money lender. For some, freedom meant freedom from the local *thanedar*, the policeman, who was seen as an agency of an oppressive state. In no case did he really see the people talking about freedom from the British as a major priority. And the reasons are very clear because there weren't very many lives upon whom the British touched directly. The British ruled through a bureaucracy, an administrative system and there weren't very many in this country at that time. At the time, at the peak of the British Empire in India there weren't more than 70 or 80,000 Europeans in this country running the empire. So the British presence was furthest from what they had in mind. What most of the people had in mind was some form of a system in which they would be allowed to act with greater sense of autonomy, a greater sense of their own right, to exercise their will.

Freedom came with considerable disorder and there was a lot of turmoil. There was a lot of violence in the air and took two years to settle down. By this time, the Constitutuent Assembly had progressed very far with its work of drafting free India's republican Constitution. Between the formal adoption of the Constitution in November 1949 and its entry into force exactly two months afterwards, there was a certain kind of upsurge in the public mood, there was a certain sense of optimism around and people suddenly began to have the sense of being free citizens. And for most Indians, it was a new sense of autonomy because they hadn't had that sense of being free citizens till then. At best, they had a notion of being subjects of a sovereign. And the difference is very clear. In any kind of a monarchy, all rights belong to the sovereign. All power is held by the sovereign and the subjects only enjoy whatever rights they have at the sufferance of the sovereign. In a republic, in contrast, citizens hold all the power which they give themselves through a constitution which is an expression of their will.

There were some who cautioned that the euphoria might be a little premature. One of them was B R Ambedkar, always a very sagacious presence in our political scene. And what he said was very clear that constitutional morality is a sentiment that is, in a sense, alien to India, that democracy is a topsoil on a deeply and fundamentally undemocratic social fabric, and that it takes a lot of effort and goodwill and good faith to cultivate a sense of constitutional morality.

So what exactly did Ambedkar mean by constitutional morality? I think in subsequent years we've been able to fill in the kind of missing gaps in his assessment, and it seems that he was referring to a state in which everybody is aware of his or her rights, but more importantly, also aware of other persons' rights. It is not just sufficient that you should be asserting your rights all the time because this could potentially bring you into collision with another person's exercise of his or her rights.

This is something that subsequent philosophical theory has dealt with in terms of the two notions of liberty, associated with the philosopher Isaiah Berlin notably. And he spoke about two kinds of liberty. There's the positive liberty and the negative liberty. Positive liberty is the right to do as your will dictates without any kind of external interference. And this could be a positive thing in some circumstances because it empowers citizens to partake of the decisions of the political sovereign. It gives them a right to have their voices heard in the decisions of the political sovereign. But it also potentially involves threats to other peoples' rights because the complete and unfettered exercise of one person's rights could potentially be an intrusion into another person's rights. The popular way of putting it is that my right to swing my arms around ends where the nose of another person begins. You may have that right, but you don't have the right to punch another person in the nose. So that applies for every kind of right you can imagine. Right to free speech, the right to a profession, the right to whatever else. So the negative liberty as conceived by Isaiah Berlin involved a zone of autonomy that every person has where no external agency can intervene, whether it is a state or any other person or the community, whatever be the system and the structure of authority within that society. There is that zone of autonomy which has to be preserved so that negative liberty can never be surrendered under any circumstances.

If you look at the phraseology and the architecture of our Constitution, there's an elaborate chapter we have on the fundamental rights. And in fact, the Indian Constitution is believed to have reproduced at least two thirds or more of the Government of India Act of 1935. The administrative part of the Constitution doesn't have very great dissimilarities with the Government of India Act of 1935. But what is fundamentally different is in the fundamental rights chapter and that is where the Constitution makers made their greatest contribution. And the phraseology of the Constitution seems to couch the fundamental rights more in the language of negative rights than positive rights.

For instance, let's look at one of the fundamental rights, which is the right to life and liberty. That's Article 21 of our Constitution. It says that nobody can be deprived of life or liberty except under process established by law. So that is a negative liberty that when you are threatening to take away the liberty of a person, there has to be a certain process of law that is followed. Take the right against arbitrary detention and arrest. Article 22 of the Constitution, which says that every person who's arrested on whatever offence has a right to legal recourse and has to be told what are the provisions of the law under which he has been charged.

There are of course several among the fundamental rights which are defined in a positive sense, such as the right to free speech, the right to freedom of conscience and so on. But all these are subject to reasonable restrictions, as we shall see.

Now over time these rights came to be diluted and that is one of the regrettable features of our evolution as an independent country; as a republic we were unable to deliver on many of those promises and these failures started right at the very inception. For instance, the right to life and liberty has been subject to numerous qualifications since then particularly in matters involving armed forces and their special powers to contain disorder or states of rebellion. There law which pertains to lives that are taken in that pursuit are invariably observed in the breach, and the mandatory statutory magisterial inquiry that should follow invariably ends up being a case of the perpetrators themselves sitting in judgement of their own actions.

Similarly, with Article 22 the right to fair trial and so on the right to be informed of the grounds on which you are being placed under arrest. Right at the very beginning there was an Article in our Constitution, Article 13 which said that any law which is in contravention of the fundamental rights chapter will stand nullified at the moment that the Constitution comes into effect. Which means that as on 26 January 1950, everybody who was in preventive detention in the entire country would stand free, discharged. But that was a situation in which the bureaucracy that had succeeded in the task of restoring order really balked because there were a number of people under detention at that time starting with people who were taken into custody under Defence of India Rules during the World War II. Then there were people who were arrested following the mutiny of 1946 and then there were lots of socialists and communists who were in detention after the events in Telangana and other parts of the country. And, I think the administration really worried that setting these people free would involve perhaps an aggravation of the state of disorder which was then more or less under control, though still a little vulnerable to a possible fresh outbreak.

So members of the Constitutional Assembly felt this was deeply repugnant to the spirit of a newly independent country seeking to establish itself as a republic of equal citizens. But the cabinet and the administration had its way. Finally, Sardar Vallabhbai Patel who was then home minister went before the Constitutional Assembly and said that he spent a sleepless night before he gave his consent to the retention of the preventive detention clauses in the Constitution. So since then the number of situations in which preventive detention is an option have multiplied. And you find it even today that there are any number of laws which permit for preventive detention and there are any number of laws which permit for detention indefinitely without any information being made available on the nature of the charges, even without legal recourse being available. And this, again is more or less a self-perpetuating power play by the Executive in which judicial scrutiny very seldom comes into the picture.

So two of the significant negative rights that the Constitution held out, have become considerably diluted over the years. There were a few others which are very important to consider and which have the language of negative rights, but which still have a positive affirmative content about them. And I'm referring here to Articles 14, 15, 16 of the Constitution, which are different in their phraseology. For instance, Article 14, which pertains to equality before the law and equal treatment under the law, applies to all persons. Article 15, which is about non-discrimination, and Article 16, which is about equal opportunity in public employment, apply only to citizens. So it's very important, especially now that we are actively engaged in this debate over amendments to the Citizenship Act, to understand that Article 14 applies to all persons. So every person who's in this country, whether as a refugee, as an immigrant, whatever, has that right to equal treatment under the law.

These provisions were challenged almost immediately. Not the Articles themselves, but under the Articles, certain administrative measures such as affirmative action, the preferential treatment for certain vulnerable sections in public employment—these were challenged. The famous case of State of Madras vs Srimathi Champakam Dorairajan (1951) and Supreme Court had no difficulty in striking down the affirmative action policies as contrary to the Equal Opportunity and Non-discrimination clauses. So this impelled the government to come up with the First Amendment, which protected the executive authority to grant special measures of preference for socially and educationally backward classes. Now, over time, this from being a negative definition of rights, became a positive affirmation, because it was read over time as a stronger affirmation of the equality principle.

The initial reading of the Supreme Court, which is a conservative reading, was that positive discrimination is an exception to the right to equality, which is a contingent kind of exception because of certain historical disadvantages that certain sections of our people have. But over time, particularly in the 1960s and 1970s when called upon to develop a deeper kind of jurisprudence over affirmative action, the Supreme Court affirmed that this is a stronger kind of statement of the right to equality, that the equal treatment of unequals is itself a perpetuation of inequality. So in a sense, it gave an extra layer of legitimacy to the affirmative action programmes of the government. So these are the ways in which our understanding, our appreciation of constitutional rights have changed over the years. And there is then one Article in the Constitution, in the fundamental rights chapter which you could say is explicitly framed as a positive right. And this is Article 19, which is called the rights to freedom Article, which pertains to the right to free speech, the right to free association, the right to free movement, the right to seek livelihood through any profession, a whole range of rights which are encapsulated in Article 19. Then of course and this is typical of our fundamental rights chapter: every such affirmation of rights is followed by what is called a non-obstante clause, which is a 'notwithstanding clause'. The format of this clause is basically that 'notwithstanding anything in the above Article, you can impose some reasonable restrictions on rights on such and such grounds'.

This has become especially contentious in the matter of the right to free speech. Nowadays the media is subject to serious intimidation if it carries critical commentary or critical reporting about people in authority.

There are formal means of intimidating them through what is called SLAPP litigation, strategic litigation against public participation, as it's called. When you can drag a media outlet to court on various kinds of frivolous charges and tie them up indefinitely, you can drain their resources. And in these times, most media houses are working on strapped budgets, they're working on shoestring budgets, and they don't have the staying power to withstand prolonged litigation in our judicial system. So this involves an implicit threat to the media. And then there are other kinds of intimidation tactics, which are through overt acts of violence, threats and intimidation. And we recently saw that newspaper, the largest circulated Hindi language newspaper, *Danik Bhaskar*, which did some amazingly penetrating coverage of excess deaths in the recent second surge of the COVID-19 pandemic, was soon afterwards raided by the income tax authorities. So that was a clear signal to them that too much assertion of your right to free speech, which is the obverse, the other side, of the public right to know, because the newspaper serves a public function of fulfilling the right to information. So these two are two sides of the same coin. This was, in a manner of speaking, a way of denying the public the kinds of rights that would enable them to be constructive participants in our civic life.

There is another category of rights which are identity specific. And I'm referring here to the right we just referred to here a little while back of affirmative action, of preferential treatment in certain kinds of public employment. And it also is inherent in the Constitution in the sense of Article 17 of the Constitution, which immediately follows the Article on Equality Before the Law, Equal Opportunity and Non-discrimination. Article 17, is an Article abolishing untouchability. Now, untouchability, you could say, is the ultimate form of discrimination you can practise. But, it is worthwhile asking the question whether, with Articles 14, 15 and 16 already in place, is it necessary to have a further affirmation of the abolition of untouchability? Because isn't that already included within the ambit of Articles 14, 15 and 16? The answer is yes, probably, if you take an expansive reading of these three Articles, the abolition of untouchability can be read into them. But the reason why there was a specific Article introduced is that the Indian Constitution in its Fundamental Rights chapter is an exercise in multiple redundancies. They say the same thing over and over again in many different ways to avoid any possible ambiguities in subsequent judicial interpretation. So that is why the abolition of untouchability is included with a specific purpose in the Fundamental Rights chapter.

Subsequently, we had the Protection of Civil Rights Act (1955) which says in its preamble that it applies to those rights covered by Article 17 of the Constitution, which means, in other words, that applies to the people once described as untouchables, once subject to the stigma of untouchability, and once subject to the kind of discrimination, the whole discriminatory treatments that were reserved for untouchables. So it doesn't mean that other people don't have civil rights. It's only that the denial of civil rights over centuries to the untouchables, to the Dalits, as they're called, was of such a magnitude that it needs very kind of concrete remedial measures for period of time which could not at that time be foreseen. And as you can see, it still continues being enforced, the special protections for the Dalit people. (Now, of course, Ambedkar had no difficulty in using the term untouchables. The term Dalits came later.)

So identity based protections were also extended to the Adivasis, the scheduled tribes as they were called. And so these are the only two identity based protections that are granted under the Constitution. Now, you can ask whether these are all that we need at this time and in recent times if you look at the kind of epidemic of vigilante violence against the religious minorities in this country, then you will realise that there is perhaps need for another kind of protective legislation which specifically includes religious minorities. And in fact, recently, two years back, when the Supreme Court was hearing a petition on this wave of lynching of people of the Muslim faith, it felt compelled to record in its official order what should have been obvious to all that lynching is a scar and a slur upon our society. And that should have been obvious to all then it wouldn't in a functioning republic or a functioning democracy, have taken the highest judicial bench to affirm that kind of virtual truism. But that's where we have reached at this time. So we could ask whether identity based protections are sufficient under our constitutional rights. I think now that question has to be faced, and has to be faced seriously and dispassionately. It's unfortunate today that all these debates are invariably drowned out by a wave of orchestrated outrage from the other side. But this is something that we really need to look at this time.

And the history behind this is that the first draft of the Constitution had section dealing specifically with minority rights, and apart from the provision of equality under the law, which in itself should be sufficient guarantee, the first draft had a provision, a separate provision on minority rights. Now you can say that one is superfluous when you have already provided for equality before the law. You don't need a specific provision on minority rights, but the Constituent Assembly believed that it was necessary and that equality, the true function, the true power of the equality clause, could only be realised if there is a concrete kind of provision for minority rights. But then there was all the dislocation of Partition that came about. And then soon afterwards, Sadar Vallabhbhai Patel came before the Constituent Assembly and said that in the changed circumstances, we don't believe that we need to really persist with this part of our Constitution. Govind Vallabh Pant, who was also a senior and influential member of the Constituent Assembly, came forth with an explicit kind of denunciation of this tendency to think in terms of communities because he said that we were not a nation of communities. We are a nation of citizens. And we should just speak in terms of an individual citizen and his or her rights, not in terms of the community and the community's collective rights. In fact, if you look at most systems of law globally, you can recognise collective rights only when they are in their violations. For instance, you can say that collectivity does not have inherent rights. Each member of that collectivity has individual rights, but the collectivity itself does not have specific rights. But you can see that when the rights of individuals belonging to that collectivity are violated and there's a persistent pattern of these violations, then you know that collective rights have some meaning in this kind of situation.

So equality before the law, I think, has remained a fictional promise. It has not yet been realised anywhere near the way it should be. And this is not unique to India. But in India, the other kinds of income and status based discrimination is also overlaid with another identity based kind of discrimination. And that is the unique kind of challenges which, in our 75-year anniversary of independence, we have to really face and address. So if the biggest challenge that we have as a nation, as we enter our 75 years of independence, is perhaps to make equality before the law a reality for everybody in this country, and that means, at the first, removing the identity based kind of discriminations that we've seen rampant over the years. Now, this is obvious that the infirmities in the law are what are creating this kind of discrimination and the sense of loss of confidence amongst other people in the processes of the law.

So obviously, the administration needs to be strengthened. But more than that, I think we need to recognise some of the warnings that Ambedkar spoke about long time back. And one was, of course, his scepticism about whether India was yet ready for claiming nationhood status because he said that we were a vast array, a vast diversity of countries and different religions and, in fact, different nationalities, and that it takes a great deal of effort to make a single seamless whole out of all this. And a second was his belief that often society practises discrimination and violates individual rights much more seriously than the state, and here he's speaking in a kind of a debate with Gandhi and Tagore and others, who spoke critically of nationalism in many senses, because of this sense of us versus them that it fostered. And Ambedkar was speaking against their perception that the way to create national solidarity is to build up the unity of civil society. And his response to that was very simple. His response to that was that often societies practise discrimination and oppression on a much greater scale than governments do. So you often need to have correctives and legal provisions that arm the government with the power to neutralise these kind of oppressions within society.

Well, what's happened in India over the last three decades perhaps, is that the government, rather than using the law to correct the inherited disparities, has been actually reinforcing these, has been drawing its strength by cultivating the fissures within civil society. So that accounts for several of the abuses we have seen in recent decades. The kind of impunity for mass violence, for instance, against minorities, whether it's Muslims or Dalits or Adivasis. We see an upsurge of it. Now, we don't see it in the sense that we used to see concentrated episodes earlier, but we see it on an everyday basis. There's a kind of recurrent pattern that you see every day. It's become a quotidian part of our lives to see these videos circulating on WhatsApp or other social media platforms, or of some kind of report which even the media often tries to shut its eyes to but often feel compelled to carry because the abuses are often so shocking and so gross.

So where do we go about finding the correctives for these things? Firstly, the administration has to be made more representative. And I think the beginnings that we have seen in terms of affirmative action should be extended to all. We need to firmly set our face against the kind of disruption that the other side causes when we talk about fair representation for all.

Now, I don't think anybody says that fair representation for all means proportionate representation in the apparatus of government, but it means that there should be a reasonable representation and a reasonable attention paid to the compulsions of equality before the law. And now, we are seeing also a kind of cultural effacement that's happening; there's a kind of denial of the full richness of our cultural heritage and a growing tendency to just ascribe it to one single kind of root going back centuries. Now, this is calculated to alienate large sections of our people, not just the religious minorities, but also the erstwhile untouchables or Dalits and Adivasis from a sense of participation in the national mainstream. And this is where our practice of secularism has itself become severely deficient because the way we've looked at this principle is in terms of equality of all and equal space for all in the public sphere. But that is not how secularism works because if you're talking about equal space for all in the public sphere, there is a tendency for majoritarianism to win and particularly it provides an incentive for majoritarian kind of politics and communal modes of political mobilisation. So a strict norm for separation of the two is necessary. I think we've made beginnings in the past, but these beginnings have often been throttled because of infirmities in our kind of philosophical convictions. The way we have set about thinking these complex issues through has been notably kind of weak. We need to strengthen our resolve and to address this issue squarely and to arrive at a kind of resolution, at least in terms of the principles. And those principles will remain weakly implemented or completely unimplemented if there isn't sufficient will in the administrative paradise.

So that's the other aspect of it which we have to attend to. And then the whole cultural offensive has to be thwarted and has to be turned back and we have to assert ourselves as a country of a very rich and diverse cultural inheritance. And for that we need stronger protections for free speech. The point now is that most people, creative artists particularly, are always looking over their shoulders trying to check out whether some creative product that they're putting out for the public is going to meet with the strict norms imposed by the thought police. So this burdens the judicial apparatus enormously. And the judicial apparatus with its current unmanageable docket of cases is obviously unable to provide timely remedies. And often it provides remedies that seek to accommodate the voices of censorship to an inordinate degree.

So these are some of the priorities that we need to look at. And the whole Fundamental Rights chapter remains integral to our identity as a republic not any kind of religion based nationalism. This is where we should be focusing our attention more and more. And ultimately, there is no gainsaying the fact that identity based discrimination flourishes on an undergirding of economic inequality, of rampant economic inequality. And this economic inequality has become so sharp in the last three decades that polarisation in society at the material level is now virtually complete. And the polarisation we're seeing at the cultural and at the social level is perhaps an epiphenomenon of this. So finally, there is no escape from the necessity to address the issue of economic equity if we are to remain true to our promises, to ourselves at the time that we adopted our republican Constitution.

Contemporary History

Voices of Dissent

Romila Thapar

I would like to talk about my recent book, *Voices of Dissent: An Essay* (2021), in which I discuss some forms of dissent from the Indian past and some of which I link with the present. I shall begin by trying to define what I mean by dissent, and then discuss two broad examples of major dissenting ideas from two past traditions. And in the latter part, I shall refer to a couple of examples of dissent that suggest a link between the comprehension of dissent in past times with some of the ways in which it has been expressed in our times.

My interest in the subject is not recent, nor was it roused primarily by increasing attempts to disallow dissenting opinion in many parts of the world today, including in our society. I have been writing on the concept of dissent in pre-modern India off and on for the last half century. I see dissent as central to social and cultural change, a centrality that is not new to history but tends to be ignored very often in the study of Indian history. Even the evolution of what we call civilisation is a process in which dissent and consent were exercised in the selection of that which is acceptable and that which is to be rejected. The selection was made by contemporary evaluation, as also by later historians. We pay little attention to these selections as debates, assuming that the process was constantly consensual.

My other purpose is to suggest that the continuity of the presence of dissent in various forms through the centuries was essential. Some characteristic forms can be recognised as having continued to be effective in present times as well, and my example of this will come from the Indian National Movement for Independence and our subsequent efforts to establish a democratic society.

Let me begin, then, by attempting to define what I mean by dissent. So, dissent stems from a difference of opinion or a disagreement, but is not arbitrary. It may begin with minor disagreement, but is recognised as dissent when it refers to a specific issue of some substance that introduces alternative ideas both in thought and in practice. Dissent, therefore, has to be directed to a matter of importance. It can be a form of protest, although protest is generally more organised. Therefore, it is better, perhaps, to say that dissent can change into or become a form of protest. A distinguishing and significant feature is that dissent is nonviolent. Dissent tends to be more vocal in what we call complex societies that bring together a variety of communities following diverse occupations, social rules and belief systems. The greater needs of variant cultures can encourage dissent among some.

Dissent is significant, for instance, to the kind of cultures that are brought together in what we call civilisations. The process of formulating the requirements of civilisation, for instance, meant selecting ideas and forms of expression, discarding some and furthering others. This interplay of conformity and dissent cannot be ignored. Dissent encourages the questioning of the world in which we live, and in this process alternatives are formulated. Any advancement in knowledge requires questioning existing knowledge. Existing explanations sometimes give way to newer and better ones. Otherwise, there is bound to be stagnation. Dissent lies at the root of philosophical discourse, as is stated more than once in Indian philosophical discussion. For example, it is said then that when making a statement of some consequences, the first step is to state clearly and at length the views of the opponent disagreeing with the proposed argument, what is referred to as the *Purvapaksha*. The second step is the refutation of this argument by the proponent, the *Pratipaksha*. And finally, there is a debate or dialogue on the two views in the hope for a solution—the *Siddhanta*. This seemingly dialectical method appears to have been practised in the debates that are referred to as taking place in royal courts, as, for instance, the debate between the Shaivas and the Buddhists at the court of Harsha, the ruler of Kanauj, in the 7th century AD.

What this procedure recognises is the centrality of dissent and the importance of dialogue in the search for a solution when dissent is registered. My examples of dissent are from the religions of pre-modern India. This is not because I think that religion is the primary area where dissent is registered, but because dissent can be seen with greater clarity in every religion. Secondly, my concern is not with dissent in theology, but in the social theories that religions construct, especially those that attract a following through explaining human existence. The explanations were diverse in modern times; however, attempts were made to bring all religious movements in India other than the Abrahamic beliefs under a single umbrella. They were seen as multiple manifestations of the same religious doctrine with few dissenting opinions. This at least was helpful in understanding them as not all conform, and many disagree. Recognising the disagreement makes them more visible and in the study of Indian religion, it is often the diverse sects of each religion that give direction to religious evolution rather than any monolithic unities that we today ascribe to them. Religious institutions reflect social values and activity, and apart from monasteries and nunneries that are distinct from society, there are institutions such as places of worship or schools of learning that contribute substantially to the actions and ethics of a society. The intersection of religious ideas and social activities often led to dissenting opinions. An example of this was the debate in one of the early Buddhist councils subsequent to the death of the Buddha on whether the *Sangha* should permit monks to accept monetary donations—a fundamental debate that all religions should discuss. The multiple sects that sprout around every religion can be expressions of deviation or dissent or can be modifications of existing forms. A sect finds its place somewhere along the spectrum. This is a different pattern from a single monotheism unified by creed and catechism. And this pluralism is characteristic of religion in India and may well relate to the particular social structures that prevail.

Let me illustrate what I am saying with a couple of examples where dissent has been crucial to the form taken by the religions.

An early articulation of this is what began as a parallel movement, but descended significantly from the established religion.

Vedic Brahmanism was the dominant religion in the earlier part of the first millennium BC. Multiple Gods were worshipped not as icons, but through elaborate sacrificial rituals that consumed much of the wealth that was produced. Its ethics drew on the belief in the reincarnation of the individual soul, what was to become the famous theory of *Karma*. This view met with dissent from what have been broadly termed as the Samana religions—the Buddhists in the main, but including the Jains and the Ajivikas. Other dissenters, the Charvaka or Lokayata, taught a firmly materialist philosophy. They all denied the existence of deities. Consequently, Vedic texts could not be taken as divinely revealed, and therefore sacred forms and locations of worship differed from the Vedic, as did the definition of reincarnation and possible liberation from it. Causal explanations were based on reason and logic, and this dissent was only broadly uniform among the Samanas, as they, too, registered degrees of disagreement among themselves. References to the Brahman-Samana confrontation are explicit in the edicts of the Mauryan King, Ashoka, who pleaded for greater tolerance and harmony between them. The period from the Mauryas to the Guptas is one in which the competition is apparent, and in the post-Gupta period, it is Brahmanism that emerges triumphant. Brahmanical writing refers to these dissenters as *Nastika*, nonbelievers, and sometimes even viewed them as heretics. The term continued to be used for them in Sanskrit texts as late as the 16th century AD.

The grammarian Patanjali compares the hostility between the Brahmanas and the Samanas to that between the snake and the mongoose. The term *Nastika* was not confined to the Samanas alone. It was extended to include all nonbelievers. Thus, in a reference from a 16th century text, *Nastikas* or nonbelievers included the Turushkas or the Turks, as applied to people from Central Asia and later to Muslims. This, of course, brings to mind the Islamic term *Kafir*. The irony was that the Turushkas did believe in God, but their

God was Allah, and not any of the Brahmanical Gods and hence, they were regarded as nonbelievers. The Samanas were *Nastikas* because they originally did not believe in any deity. Buddhism had its own dissenters. A significant dichotomy separated the Hinayana and the Mahayana sects when they interpreted the teachings of the Buddha in the first millennium AD. It met with conditions different from what it had known in the subcontinent, and this led to fresh questions, new answers, and quite often, the founding of a new sect. The degree of demarcation from the existing religious order was variable.

The success of a religion depends on its relationship with society, and particularly with those in authority and the elite who provide the patronage and the donations for rituals. A popular following gives it a different kind of support, and the Samanas had to compete for patronage to establish their social base. But monastic institutions establishing an alternative system were dependent on society. Vedic Brahmanism had a wealthy, prestigious, and generally elite patronage. The popular religion that grew out of these beginnings was what is now being called by scholars of Hinduism as *Puranic* Hinduism. It did not formally descend from Vedic Brahmanism, but left it to its own Brahmanical devices. *Puranic* Hinduism gave prominence to certain newer deities and forms of worship like the deities of the Vaishnava, the Shaiva, and the Shakta traditions. Under these labels, it also included many local cults, but the focus was always on deity. One among the many deities had prominence, and the remaining deities were either absent or were marginal in Vedic worship. Each of the major deities of *Puranic* Hinduism were maintained by distinctive sects with distinctive texts such as the *Purana*.

Variations within the sects had a large range origin and myths and rituals were recorded, irrespective of whether the deities were old or even very recent. Like most religions, *Puranic* Hinduism had both a gentle side with close human manifestations of deities that the worshipper was comfortable with, as also the more wrathful, angry manifestation of deities. In some forms, they became icons of love, devotion, and passion and compassion, the emotions that guided their worship. One might ask whether this emphasis also drew partly from the Samana tradition, with little emphasis on deity, as well as the Bhakti tradition, which endorsed this gentler side. Hindu institutions were parallel to, but different from those of the Samanas. Temples replaced Chaityas, sometimes literally, and often became places of pilgrimage, thereby attracting commercial activities as well. Icons of the deities were introduced with elaborate rituals, some invented afresh. The monastery was, as yet, alien to Brahminism, although something echoing it, like the matha, became a focus of propagation. The renouncer, by contrast, became a monk or a nun, but continued to have limited links with society. And in this, the renouncer is different from the ascetic, who was ideally self-exiled and lived in isolation. Renunciation was central to Samanism as it was the path to *Niravana*. It involved dissent from Brahmanical teaching, opting out of social obligations, and adopting an alternative monastic life focusing on self-liberation or *Moksha*.

However, it was not self-isolation, since contact with society was necessary. The monk had to collect his food as alms from people in the vicinity, and his concern about their well-being was required by the teaching. Violence was disallowed. It can be seen as a reciprocal relationship with society, one that was new and different from what had existed before. The practice of renunciation was implicit in the image of what came to be called as the man who heals, performs miracles, meditates, and is helpful in misfortune, the man whom we today call the 'holy man'. He is not the priest. He lives distanced from society, but wanders through villages and towns and as an icon, his choice of being a holy man could be used effectively, but could also be abused in giving direction to a community. The later incoming religions brought new ideas. These could either create dissent or be amalgamated into new practices and beliefs.

The mixing and the merging of new religious ideas takes shape, for instance, with the coming of various forms of Islam. We refer to this event as starting with the Arabs invading Sindh in the 8th century AD. But in fact, their more effective and long lasting entry was as traders all down the west coast of India in Gujarat to Kerala in the South. The religious mix that emerged took the form of new socio-religious sects in origin, drawing from both *Puranic* Hinduism and Islam, but not conforming to either and evolving independently. These sects are mostly the early Bohras, Khojas, Mappilas, Navayats and such like. The Central Asian presence was intensified at historical moments through invasion, but it was actually more firmly established with migration and settlement. Various schools of Sufi sects spread their version of Islam with their diverse ideas and practices, dissenting from or borrowing from existing religions in India. One of the most interesting examples of this were the borrowings between the Nath Yogis and the Sufis in the Punjab. This is one explanation as to why the proponents of Krishna Bhakti, that is, devotees of the deity Krishna, the incarnation of Vishnu, were not only Hindus such as Vallabhacharya and Surdas, but also came from well-placed Muslim families. Syed Ibrahim Khan or Raskhan and Abdul Rahim Khan-i-Khanan or Rahim are among those who composed Dohas (couplets) in Hindi in praise of Krishna and Radha. The verses are still sung as bandishes in Hindustani classical music. Such devotees were treated as dissenters by the proponents of orthodoxy in both religions, by both the Kazis, the Mullahs and the Maulavis as well as the Pundits and the Brahmanas. Bhakti, thus, as a form of religion, had multiple nuclei all over the subcontinent. Their verses were devotional and by implication were often full of social comments.

In our times, these multiple sects have been treated as part of one unified monolithic religious movement. They were actually diverse and responded to specific local, religious, and regional requirements. They were not defining a subcontinental religion. Each Bhakti sant worshipped one deity of choice in his or her own way, with or without rituals and often through songs, hymns and narratives in the local language. There was, therefore, an obvious diversity geared to the local region, although there were a few broad similarities. Either the deities differed or if the same one was worshipped, it was done in another way and of course in another language. So, the nuances were not the same. We may well ask why there was a difference? Generally, little or no mention is made of other Bhakts from distant places. Neither Kabir nor Mirabai for example, mention the Alvars or the Nayanars of the Tamil speaking region. For some sants, the worship of the deity was paramount, but for others it was the message of social equality. Implicit in his devotion, Ravidas describes his utopia not as a paradise, but as the imagined city of Begumpura, the city where there is no sorrow, given the absence of inequality.

Social equality is also asserted in the ritual of organised pilgrimages among some sects and those congregating in devotion are all treated as of equal status. This breaks two of the fundamental rules of caste—they eat together, and there is no prohibition on touching during the period of pilgrimage and the rules of the *Dharmashastra* do not apply. Even in those religions that preached equality of all, social difference was marked and treated as necessary. The separation between acceptable castes and the lower castes and untouchables was in practice. Across religions, places of worship or areas within the normal places of worship were demarcated and segregated. We also need to inquire into the forms of dissent that the excluded castes, the avaranas, Dalits as we call them today, may have adopted, although not perhaps openly so. Let me repeat that dissent was always present as an undercurrent in the ideas and movements associated with many aspects of life. Barring the orthodox, religion, at all social levels was malleable and adjusted either visibly or invisibly to social and political change, as is evident from the histories of the sects. There is, for instance, much mutation and reformulation of religions in colonial times, and the presence of dissent needs greater recognition, especially in times of historical change. What have been called socio religious reform movements in the 19th century, the Brahmo Samaj, the Arya Samaj, the Prarthana Samaj, and such like, were inevitably imprinted with some colonial ideas. They questioned Brahmana orthodoxy, but with the intention of suggesting reform rather than any heterodox replacement. The Arya Samaj, for instance, reconstructed Vedic society as a utopia and propagated returning to Vedic values and practices. Calls for returning to tradition often draw on a virtually invented tradition in accord with the ideological and social needs of present times. Nationalism is one such invention and it emphasised the emergence of a new socio-political structure, namely a nation state. Some advocated it as a new utopia, that of a secular democratic state, others reversed this by imagining a future state identified with the majority religion as its most significant feature.

Democratic nationalism was a protest against colonial rule, articulated in various ways of dissent and converted into a manifestation of social and political protest. In the early twentieth century it was a part of the anti-colonial secular national movement for independence. The question I am asking is, was it an entirely new experience for the Indian people? The protest incorporating degrees of dissent attracted a large number of people who became supporters of secular nationalism. This nationalism was distinct from the nascent but growing religious nationalisms, the Muslim and the Hindu. These had a different agenda and teleology. Their intention was to establish religious majoritarian states. These two religious nationalisms took their cue from the colonial understanding of Indian history and consequently could not and did not confront colonial power. Their ideas were based on colonial thinking. Religious nationalism, by its very premise, cannot accommodate democracy as primacy is always given to a particular category of citizens, usually based on religion, but it could also depend on their ethnicity or language. Religious nationalism and democracy are in conflict but the secular national movement, envisaging a democratic nation state, took forward some of these ideas of dissent.

As had been formulated in earlier times, these were more in keeping with the requirements of groups protesting against colonial rule. A few earlier forms of dissent surfaced again. Among them were two that were adapted by Gandhi as among his forms of protest. One was the 'Dharna' or the hunger strike, and the other was what he called *Satyagraha*. His awareness of deliberately adapting the earlier forms of dissent and protest is being researched. Mine is just a hint, a possible glance in that direction. What I am arguing in this discussion of dissent is that we should look more closely at the links between the past and the present.

One among the many reasons for the success of these forms of dissent in the 20th century may have been that the Indian people were familiar with these forms as a recognised articulation of dissent. Where Gandhi resorts to fasts to make a political demand either from the colonial power or from competing nationalisms, he is projected as an independent person with the stature of a Mahatma, literally, the great soul. In effect, rather similar to the holy man that I was talking about earlier. He takes it upon himself to speak for the people of India in supporting their demand for freedom and to live in harmony, else he could lose his life by fasting as symbolic of dissent. He needed the stature to take this position. This was recognised both by the Indian people and by the colonial power, directly or indirectly. Gandhi's major formulation of a method of dissent which became associated with him was what he called *Satyagraha*, literally, holding the truth. The creation of this form of dissent drew partly and perhaps subconsciously from a tradition of dissent that prevailed in many cultures of India and which I have referred to earlier.

Thus, I would argue that *Satyagraha* was a form of dissent that evoked older practices in a modern situation and without consciously linking it to older forms. It can be called dissent, since it has characteristics familiar to the Indian people recalled by the continuing presence of the Renouncers, the Bhakti Sants, the Jogis, the Peers and Fakirs and other categories—people who are often called holy men, or the ones who opt to stay out of the society. The iconic use of the phrase, 'the half-naked fakir', for Gandhi evoked unintentionally the established tradition of dissenters. All of the latter claimed the right to deny their consent to what existed if they so wished. Dissent is not just disagreement. Its intention has an objective. The objective in South Africa was not identical with the one in India. Nevertheless, dissent is directed towards political and social change and ensuring the well-being of people.

This makes it reminiscent of the aims of the earlier dissenters, the Samanas and the Bhakti Sants. It does not merely advocate a return to the vague fantasy of a golden age. It defines that age, even if differently. It endorses a dialogue between opposite opinions in order to arrive at a solution reminiscent of the method suggested in early times for solving opposing arguments. It speaks to and includes all and every citizen of a nation, men and women. It is specifically not majoritarianism. Implicit in its thinking is the need for the foundation of a society to be democratic. It is irrespective of religion, of caste, or of status. Women are encouraged to participate. The presence of women is particularly striking, as indeed, it was in the earlier movements of dissent. It was the Samanas that permitted women to take up renunciation as nuns. Admittedly, after some debate and persuasion, women sants like Andal, Meera, Lal Ded were accepted as teachers. It is often forgotten that the confined condition of women as advocated in the *Dharmashastra* texts is not what was advocated in all texts and practices in past times. Many were different, whatever be the degree of difference. The national movement did not necessarily treat all women as liberated citizens but it was a realisation that if dissent is to be effective as passive resistance, it must be the voice of both men and women.

The Soul-Satyagraha was one such. It would be worth knowing in greater detail how such events were given form, who participated, and why apart from the call of the Mahatma, it is equally important to ascertain the reaction of the participants as to how they understood the essential meaning of such activities. After 1947, passive resistance on any subcontinental scale has not been used when disagreeing with the laws of any government. Nevertheless, sporadic expressions of dissent have been and can be the reason for arrest, as has happened earlier under colonial governance and continues to this day. What comes to mind, however, are the two recent events of Shaheen Bagh (15 December 2019 to 24 March 2020) and the farmers protest in the vicinity of Delhi (2020-2021). Shaheen Bagh and the protests linked to it in other cities had a larger component of women and students expressing their opposition to the proposed Citizenship Amendment Bill debarring some categories of people from having citizenship in India. The overwhelming presence of women, particularly Muslim women was deeply significant. It was women opposing patriarchy and gender discrimination and the rules of orthodoxies. In endorsing the Constitution, these women were also stating their support for secularism and democracy.

The farmers' protest was against newly formulated laws (September 2020) on agricultural produce. The protesters were nonviolent, in both cases demanding a dialogue on the recently passed laws and their future. This also ties into the bigger question inherent to decisions in a democracy as to how these laws were being received by those most closely affected by them. In a democratic society, it is not only the lawmakers whose voice is to be heard, but those who are affected by the law, their voices and reactions should also be heard. Dissenting views today have a new dimension. We are no longer a colony ruled by a coloniser. We have been aspiring to function as a nation state, that is, as a secular democracy. In this context, protests can also be viewed as a comment on the questions being raised in discussions in many places. Do we need to fine tune the concept of democracy to prevent it being derailed, as is feared that this is happening in some situations? Inevitably, the wider aspects of democracy have to be discussed, such as additional ways of debating disagreement and finding solutions to the problems that we are facing today. Does elected representation suffice in conveying what people want? How, for example, can we strengthen the institutions that protect democracy? Can the three constitutional pillars, the legislature, the executive, and the judiciary be made more secure and autonomous, especially as guardians of the rights of citizens? Such questions are pertinent in the context of how democracy should function now and in the future. The failures in democratic functioning in the past century, with authoritarian systems and dictatorships coming to power in parts of Europe and Asia like in Italy, Germany, Russia, China had disastrous consequences for humanity. The repetition of that pattern is not called for *siddhanta*. One may ask as to what Gandhi would have said to recent forms of passive resistance. A distinction between the colonial situation and that in an independent nation state should be evident when it comes to the role of dissent. The passive resistance of Gandhi asserted dissent and evolved into protest.

In some polities across the world today, dissent is treated as an anti-national act. Yet, it is well established that the pivot of a liberal secular democracy is a wide-ranging debate prior to decisions which has to come to terms with dissenting views. Let me repeat what our philosophy from the past maintains; there can be no *Siddhanta* or solution if the views of the *Purvapaksha*, the opponent, are silenced by the *Pratipaksha*, the proponent. The articulation of the dialogue and debate between the two is absolutely essential. Let me say in conclusion, therefore, that it is imperative that we understand the historical centrality of dissent. It was and is essential to the formulating of culture and to the establishing of democratic forms and norms. We have to recognise the inevitability of dissent in the events that shaped our history and that are now shaping the present.

Through the Lens of the Mahatma

Mridula Mukerjee

Let us imagine how Gandhi ji would have reacted if he were present in India today. I think it is a difficult task to put Gandhi ji in today's world that is far removed from the times in which he lived, and to try and visualise how he would look at India around him. What would Gandhi ji identify as the main issues which are before us today? How would he identify what is troubling and tormenting the poor of India? How would Gandhi ji imagine what the women of India are thinking? How would he imagine what the peasants of India are thinking? And how would he then formulate an agenda for action? How would he then think of what would be the best methods, what would be the best ways of going forward and expressing those urges, expressing those needs, and trying to find solutions to those problems?

This is a rather tough task that we are setting before ourselves today. Let's see what we can make of it. Obviously, we would have to base ourselves on what we know about Gandhi ji's contribution, both at the level of ideas as well as at the level of practice, because as he said, 'My life is my message.'[1] So, more than anything else, we have to look at the man in action. Of course, we would do that through his words and through other people's perceptions of him, and then we would try and, in a way, transport that into an imagination for today.

I have identified a few issues which I think would have been of major concern and attention for Gandhi ji. The first one would be the issue of the independence and the sovereignty of India, especially as expressed in the foreign policy, economic policy, international trade and economic relationships with other powers. The second issue that I would like to take up is that of the state of democracy and civil liberties today, and how he would react to what is going on and the solutions that he would have provided. The third issue that I would like to talk about is the ideal of an inclusive India. Gandhi ji believed that all those who lived in India had a right to be its citizens, full citizens. So, how would he look at what's been going on around us today? How would Gandhi ji look at the Citizenship (Amendment) Act, 2019 (CAA)? How would he look at the National Register of Citizens (NRC)? How would he situate himself as the architect of resistance? What advice would he have for the women who fought against the CAA and the NRC, the students who were in that agitation, the farmers who sat on the borders of Delhi? How would he look at the way we have been using draconian legislation to put people behind bars? I would also like to see how he would translate his pro-poor agenda into today's India. Because the state of India's poor was of utmost concern to him and they were at the heart of his politics and struggle. How would he react to the marginalisation of the poor that we are seeing around us? How would he have reacted to the migrant workers going home under the lockdown, the rise in prices, crony capitalism?

As we know, Gandhi ji spent a lot of his life addressing the issues of untouchability and caste-based discrimination. I think he's the only person in Indian history to have carried on what became famous as the *Harijan* Tour (1933-34), where for nine months continuously, he toured the country—village by village, *mohalla* by *mohalla*, town by town, city by city—by every possible mode of transport, including by boat and on foot, to raise the issue of untouchability. How would he view the issue of women's rights and their position in India? What would be his take on the condition of the environment? After all, he had remarked, 'We have sufficient for everybody's needs, not for greed.'[2]

Gandhi ji stands for resistance, resistance to all kinds of oppression, all kinds of discrimination, all kinds of un-freedom. So, what would be his take today? Would he be happy that somewhere what he had taught has been learned by people or would he have some more advice to give?

I shall begin with the issues of independence and sovereignty. Let me take the example of the Afghanistan takeover by the Taliban (1996). The news of the takeover and America's eventual retreat burst onto our TV screens, newspapers, and every possible mode of communication. But what are we seeing? I find that India has no voice. We were silent. We were among the first to pick up our bags and vacate our embassy in Afghanistan. We didn't even stay long enough to help the Indian nationals evacuate. And where are we in terms of influencing anything that's going on in the world? I think Gandhi ji would be extremely perturbed about this. He would be extremely concerned about this because even before we became free, India had a voice in international affairs. We had our opinions about everything, whether it was Fascism in Europe or whether it was Racism in the US or whether it was the Apartheid in South Africa. After all, Gandhi ji himself spent 20 years or more of his life struggling against racial discrimination in Africa. So, he understood international issues very well. I think he would have wanted us to put in place a strong and independent foreign policy, something that our country practised under the guidance of Jawaharlal Nehru. But today on Afghanistan, we are not even called to the high table. There was a time when despite our poverty, India was in the thick of things. Whether it was Vietnam, the Korean War, the UN forces being sent to different places in Congo, India always had an opinion on and role in all such matters.

Years ago, when troubles started in Afghanistan, there was an attempt to overthrow the progressive government. And then finally at one point, the Soviet Union came in to support that progressive government (December 1979) and there was a lot of turmoil. I still remember Indira Gandhi taking a position, even though we were friends with the Soviet Union. She took an independent position and said, 'I don't think we supported the [soviet] action. We are trying to find a way so that the situation does not escalate further.'[3] All I am saying is that we had an independent voice, and that was a result of the struggle that had been led primarily at the helm by Gandhi ji.

Today, Gandhi ji would have wanted us to have our independent voice and sovereignty. He wouldn't have wanted us to become junior partners to anybody—the US, the UK or China or Russia. Similarly, I think that our economic agenda is being dictated by the interests of the multi-nationals and even at times, by countries other than our own. Gandhi ji would have definitely wanted us to become *Aatma Nirbhar* in the true sense of its term rather than just talk about it.

Democracy and civil liberties would be a major concern to Gandhi ji; let me begin by quoting him to show how deep his conviction was for civil liberties and democracy. Writing in early 1922, he said,

> Liberty of speech means that it is unassailed even when the speech hurts; liberty of the Press can be said to be truly respected only when the Press can comment in the severest terms upon and even misrepresent matters, protection against misrepresentation or violence being secured not by an administrative gagging order, not by closing down the Press but by punishing the real offender, leaving the Press itself unrestricted. Freedom of association is truly respected when assemblies of people can discuss even revolutionary projects, the State relying upon the force of public opinion and the civil police, not the savage military at its disposal, to crush any actual outbreak of revolution that is designed to confound public opinion and the state representing it. The fight for *Swaraj* means a fight for this threefold freedom before all else.[4]

Given his definition of freedom of assembly, as cited above, 'when assemblies of people can discuss even revolutionary projects', certainly he would not have approved of the way UAPA has been used in the Bhima Koregaon Case (2018), how people who have not even engaged in revolutionary projects have been put behind bars. The only line that Gandhi ji drew was that of non-violence. I quote, 'Civil liberty consistent with the observance of non-violence is the first step towards *Swaraj*. It is the foundation of freedom. And there is no room there for dilution or compromise. It is the water of life. I have never heard of water being diluted.'[5]

And how did he put these ideas into practice? How did he treat those with whom he had ideological and political differences? It's not just a question of statements of faith in civil liberties, but also about defending people with whom one does not agree. Defending your opponents, defending people with whom you may have sharp differences—not just allowing them to exist or speak—but actually coming out and defending their right to speech. I would like to just give one short example—when the Quit India movement was about to be launched and there was this meeting in the Gowalia Tank in Bombay, on 8 August 1942, that passed the resolution that Gandhi ji would be given the authority to start a movement, a few communists, who were members of the All India Congress Committee, got up and objected to it. They said that they would not agree to this because they have a different understanding of the international situation and that they felt that going against the British government would harm the international cause against fascism. But the atmosphere in Bombay was surcharged in favour of the Quit India movement. Naturally, there was some kind of hostility towards the opposing group. But Gandhi ji took to the floor and gave a speech in which he said,

> I congratulate you on the resolution that you have just passed. I also congratulate the three comrades on the courage they have shown in pressing their amendments to a division, even though they knew that there was an overwhelming majority in favour of the resolution, and I congratulate the thirteen friends who voted against the resolution. In doing so, they had nothing to be ashamed of. For the last twenty years we have tried to learn not to lose courage even when we are in a hopeless minority and are laughed at. We have learned to hold on to our beliefs in the confidence that we are in the right. It behaves us to cultivate this courage of conviction, for it ennobles man and

> raises his moral stature. I was, therefore, glad to see that these friends had imbibed the principle which I have tried to follow for the last fifty years and more.[6]

What was he doing with this statement? Gandhi ji was throwing a protective cover around the opposing communists who were obviously going to be the butt of ridicule and could even be subjected to physical attacks by the crowd. By coming out in their support of them and by admiring their courage, Gandhi ji actually stood for the ideals of liberty. And as far as democracy is concerned, I think he always emphasised that democracy is about dialogue and not a question of numbers or majorities. Democracy means you must listen to opponents and to those who differ with you. But what is happening today? Our farmers are shouting loudly for the last nine months (New Delhi, 2020-2021) but there is no dialogue. But Gandhi ji even called the revolutionaries, who believed in violence, for a dialogue and urged them to keep their violent methods at bay for some time and let him try his method of non-violence. And would you believe it? During the time of the non-cooperation movement, the revolutionaries actually suspended their methods. Probably Gandhi ji would have advised both the rulers and the rebels of today to engage in dialogue because no society can exist without dialogue.

One of the biggest problems that Gandhi ji would see in the country today is the polarisation that has been literally injected into our social and political life, where, on the grounds of religion, people are being pushed into rallying against each other. Gandhi ji would certainly set an agenda in trying to handle this problem.

As an example, I am quoting from Gandhi ji's speech on 8 August 1942, just before the Quit India movement, where he says,[7]

> Those Hindus who, like Dr. Moonje and Shri Savarkar, believe in the doctrine of the sword may seek to keep the Mussalmans under Hindu domination. I do not represent that section. I

> represent the Congress. You want to kill the Congress which is the goose that lays golden eggs. If you distrust the Congress, you may rest assured that there is to be perpetual war between the Hindus and the Mussalmans, and the country will be doomed to continue warfare and bloodshed... Congressmen will sacrifice their lives in order to protect the Mussalman against a Hindu's attack and vice versa. It is a part of their creed, and is one of the essentials of non-violence.

This was the strength with which Gandhi ji believed in an inclusive India, in Hindu-Muslim unity, in lack of polarisation, in the right of everybody to live in this land. It is all their homeland. So you can well imagine what kind of agenda he would set for us today, and how pained he would be by what is going on.

I think the issue of women's rights and position and the discrimination against women is important and has to be part of any political agenda that we formulate today. So I think we must know how Gandhi ji would have imagined the agenda today as he was uncompromising in the matter of women's rights. I quote, 'I am uncompromising in the matter of women's rights. In my opinion she should labour under no legal disability not suffered by men. I should treat the daughters and sons on a footing of perfect equality.'[8]

Rajkumari Amrit Kaur tells us[9] that Gandhi ji discarded with contempt anyone who argued with him on the basis of what *Manu* has supposedly said about women—that there can be no freedom for them. Such sayings or texts were not sacrosanct to him at all. Gandhi ji rejected them. He paid equal attention and gave equal place to girls and women in his ashram. There was an air of freedom and self-confidence in the girls and women that lived under his care, whether it was Sewa Gram or Sabarmati Ashram. Nothing delighted him more than the success of women in any sphere of life. We are told by the women inmates of the ashram that Gandhi ji paid equal attention and let equal weight to the views of women workers. I quote again,

> To call woman the weaker sex is a libel; it is man's injustice to women. If by strength is meant brute strength, then, indeed, is woman less brute than man. If by strength is meant moral power, then woman is immeasurably man's superior.[10]

So we can well imagine that he would set a very radical agenda for the women's cause today.

On the issue of environment, I am convinced that Gandhi ji would make it a crucial part of the political agenda before the people today, because he was deeply concerned about the way industrial capitalism had built on the principle of consumption. And he was convinced that the world just cannot survive if it went on like this. He would have been, I think, a prime green politician if he was alive today.

Similarly, on the issue of caste discrimination, I think we should have no doubt that he would have taken a clear-cut stand that it is high time that caste discrimination whatever there is of whatever kind, must end. There are various kinds of views about Gandhi ji on the issue of caste. Some people feel B R Ambedkar was more radical. Some people feel Gandhi ji didn't have the right answer. The issue is not who had the right answers. The issue is whether you agree that it must be on the agenda. And, then of course, there can be differences. There can be debates over what is the best way. Is reservation the best way to ensure that the downtrodden castes go forward? What kind of support do we need? Do we need other kinds of solutions? Is resistance important? Are movements important? After all, Gandhi ji led movements against 'Untouchability' and ending of caste discrimination. He encouraged inter-caste marriage in his Ashram. So whatever it is, my point is that Gandhi ji would certainly put it on the agenda because it had been put on the agenda of the freedom struggle at that time.

And finally, I would like to end with Gandhi ji's solution. After putting things on the agenda, his solution or his advice or his prescription of how to take that agenda forward would be to rely on resistance. His understanding was that when you see discrimination and oppression, it is your obligation to resist. If you do not resist, you are complicit with the oppressor. There is no midway, silence or distance is not an answer. This is what he called *Satyagraha*, the heart and soul of which is resistance. For Gandhi ji, it was not an abstract philosophical concept, but it was a weapon that was forged in the flame of struggle and sharpened on the wet stone of hard political practice. Resistance to any form of wrongdoing or un-freedom, whether it is racism, communalism, caste oppression, patriarchy, denial of democracy, inequity or economic deprivation bounded only by the limits set by non-violence was of paramount importance to him. Look how the women and the youth took up courage and fought in the anti-CAA and anti-NRC movement that began in 2019. And if it hadn't been for the lockdown (from 24 March 2020), we don't know what would have happened in this movement. If ever there was a truly Gandhian movement, in my opinion, the one direction in which Gandhi ji would point our attention, he would say, look at what's actually going on. Look at the movements of resistance that are going on today in India. Learn from them, build on them, consolidate them. And he would point our attention first and foremost to the movement that emerged against the CAA and the NRC. The women and the youth of India were in the forefront of that movement to a large extent. It was a spontaneous movement. People were their own leaders. Just at Gandhi ji had told the people of India in 1942, every man will be his own leader, 'do or die' was the slogan which he gave. But there were very few directions on what you were supposed to do, but do something or die in the attempt. Gandhi ji would definitely point to the movement of the farmers, of the peasants, which has been now going on for almost a year, nine months. They've sat at the doors of Delhi. But even before that, from July 2021 onwards when the legislation was passed, this movement has been going on, again, a movement with a decentralised local leadership, but a very powerful movement nonetheless, just as various sections of the national movement and peasant movements during that time of the freedom struggle such as the one at Bardoli in 1928. Gandhi ji would point to these and would advise us to build our strategy of resistance to the un-freedom we are experiencing, to the evil, oppression and polarisation that we are seeing around us.

Resistance begets resistance. The more people lose their fear, the more others around them lose their fear. And that's how Gandhi ji developed all his mass movements—he turned a mass of frightened, demoralised, illiterate and poor people of India into a fire fighting force which could defeat the biggest Empire in the world. And that's what he would say to you—If we could do it, if we could defeat the biggest Empire in the world, surely you too can defeat fascism today. You just have to have faith and the courage and go forward.

NOTES

1 Dharmadhikari, C S, Justice, 'Mahatma Gandhi: My Life is My Message', *Special Service and Features*, New Delhi: Press Information Bureau, Government of India, 29 September 2016, https://pib.gov.in/newsite/printrelease.aspx?relid=151237
2 Gandhi, M K, *Trusteeship*, Kelekar, Ravindra (ed.), Ahmedabad: Navajivan Trust Publication, 1960, p.3
3 11 January 1980; see: *The Washington Post*, 18 January 1980
4 *Collected Works of Mahama Gandhi* (*CWMG*), Volume 22, pp.176-77
5 Karachi Resolution of the All India Congress Committee on Fundamental Rights (1931), drafted by Jawaharlal Nehru, in consultation with Gandhi ji, was moved for adoption by Gandhi ji, *CWMG*, Volume 45, pp.370-71
6 *CWMG*, Volume 76, p.384
7 *CWMG*, Volume 76, pp.388-91
8 'The Collected Works of Mahatma Gandhi (May-August 1924)', Read Books, 2006, Vol. 5, p.340
9 *Eminent Parliamentarians Monograph Series*, New Delhi: Lok Sabha Secretariat, 1993
10 *Young India* [Weekly Journal], 10 April 1930

Jawaharlal Nehru: A Reappraisal for Today's Times

Aditya Mukherjee

It is necessary today to do a reappraisal of Jawaharlal Nehru in the present context. What happened to his vision? What can we learn from him in meeting our current challenges? These are some of the questions I will try to engage with.

Engaging with these issues is important in itself but also because these are days of demonising Nehru using all kinds of lies and abuse using the massive propaganda machinery of the Rashtriya Swayamsevak Sangh (RSS) and the Bharatiya Janata Party (BJP) which today has state power in the centre and in many states. Nehru is blamed for all of India's problems, from the Partition of the country, the Pakistan problem, the China problem, the crisis in Indian agriculture, the Kashmir issue, crisis in the educational system, the persistence of poverty, the growing religious polarisation in recent years to almost any problem facing the country today. This, nearly 50 years after his passing away! Nehru is said to be actually a Muslim, as if being a Muslim itself is a crime. Such is the hatred spread about him that one BJP leader, as reported in an RSS journal went to the extent of saying that Nathuram Godse should have aimed his gun at Nehru as he was such an evil person.[1] Apart from spreading lies about him, the effort is to also erase his memory from the minds of the Indian people. In Rajasthan, it was reported that textbooks for school children were created during the BJP regime which while talking of the Indian independence movement had no mention of Jawaharlal Nehru. The Indian Council for Historical Research (ICHR), not to be left behind in pushing the BJP government initiative, recently put up a poster celebrating the 75th Year of Indian Independence where the pictures of many freedom fighters were put up but Jawaharlal Nehru was absent and V D Savarkar was added, a person who apologised slavishly to the British promising total loyalty to them and after his release not only accepted a generous pension from the British Government but cooperated with the government and did much to weaken the freedom struggle.

Not even the British, whose chief ally the communal forces in India were, demonise Nehru in this manner, this despite Nehru spending 30 years of his life fighting the British, 9 of those years spent in British jails.

We may ask ourselves the question that if Jawaharlal Nehru was such a bad and incompetent person, why did the father of the nation, Mahatma Gandhi choose *him* as his successor and not his other brilliant comrades like C Rajagopalachari or Sardar Vallabhbhai Patel?

In a speech at the All India Congress Committee (AICC) meeting at Wardha on 15 June 1942 Gandhi ji declared:

> ...Somebody suggested that Pandit Jawaharlal and I were estranged. This is baseless...You cannot divide water by repeatedly striking it with a stick. It is just as difficult to divide us. I have always said that not Rajaji, nor Sardar Vallabhbhai but Jawahar will be my successor...When I am gone...he will speak my language too...Even if this does not happen, I would at least die with this faith.[2]

Why did Gandhi ji have such tremendous faith in Jawaharlal Nehru? One can surmise at least two reasons.

First, Jawaharlal Nehru quintessentially represented and fought for all the core values of the Indian freedom struggle which have in short been called 'The Idea of India'. These core values were in brief:

1 Sovereignty, i.e., India will be independent and self-reliant.
2 Democracy, i.e., India will be a democratic country with adult franchise with *equal rights* to all citizens, irrespective of their

caste, class, language, gender, region or ethnicity.

3 Secularism, i.e., people belonging to different religious faiths will have equal rights in the country. India will *not* be a majoritarian Hindu state. Secularism and democracy were seen as coterminous; one could not exist without the other. The term secular-democracy was often used conjointly, just as communalism was with loyalism.

4 Pro-poor orientation. Beginning from the early nationalists like Dadabhai Naoroji whose book was titled 'Poverty and Un-British Rule in India' to Gandhi ji turning the face of the country towards the poor, the *Daridranarayan*, to the socialists and communists all were agreed on a pro-poor orientation even if there was no consensus on socialism or communism.

5 Modern scientific outlook was to be propagated (what Nehru called the scientific temper) overcoming obscurantism and blind faith.

It must be noted that there was a consensus among the entire spectrum of the Indian national movement on these core values whatever may have been their other differences. From the early nationalists like Naoroji, Ranade, Gokhale to Tilak, C R Das to Bhagat Singh and other revolutionaries to Gandhi ji, Nehru, Patel, Subhash Bose, the socialists like Acharya Narendra Dev and Jayaprakash Narayan and communists like EMS Namboodiripad, Harkishan Singh Surjeet and P C Joshi, all agreed on the above core values of the 'Idea of India'. Only the loyalists and the communalists of all hues were opposed to them.

Not only did Jawaharlal Nehru fight for these values during the freedom struggle but he played a stellar role in *implementing* these ideas in the new born state after independence. Gandhi ji, perhaps anticipated this capacity of Nehru in choosing him as his successor. In fact, the burden of implementing these ideas fell largely on Nehru's shoulders with the Mahatma being murdered by a Hindu communalist within 6 months of India gaining independence and

Sardar Patel passing away in 1950. Nehru performed this task with great élan and imagination as India's first Prime Minister for about 17 years.

It is on Nehru's role in implementing the five core values of the 'Idea of India' listed above, after independence, that I will focus on today. It is necessary to do so as each element of the 'Idea of India' is deeply threatened today.

When we evaluate Nehru's role in implementing the 'Idea of India' after independence, we must remind ourselves of what economists call the 'initial conditions' from which he had to start, to get an idea of the gigantic task ahead of him at independence. Rabindranath Tagore, shortly before his death had graphically anticipated the condition of India at the end of British rule. He said:

> The wheels of fate will someday compel the English to give up their Indian empire. What kind of India will they leave behind, what stark misery? When the stream of their centuries' administration runs dry at last, what a waste of mud filth will they leave behind them.[3]

The 'mud and filth left behind' was a famine ridden country (three million perished in a man-made famine just four years before independence), where per capita income and food grain output was actually shrinking annually for the past three decades before independence, where average life expectancy at independence was a shocking low of about 30 years, 84 per cent of all Indians and 92 per cent women were illiterate. On top of all this, the British left the country deeply divided on religious lines, with millions dead and rendered homeless in a communal carnage that happened under colonial tutelage.

It was a gigantic task indeed to lift India out of this misery following the path laid down by our freedom fighters in their imagination of independent India. Nehru evolved a brilliant multi-pronged strategy to lift India out of this morass, which in fact, became an example for numerous other countries which gained independence from the colonial rule.

I

SECULARISM AND THE COMMUNAL CHALLENGE

The biggest challenge came at the time of independence itself, in the form of religious communalism threatening the secular Idea of India. India faced a holocaust like situation between 1946 and 1948. Beginning with the Calcutta killings in August 1946, the Noakhali killings and in retaliation the Bihar killings a few months later, the Partition riots leaving at least 5 lakhs dead and 60 lakhs refugees and ultimately the murder of the Mahatma on 30 January 1948 by Godse, a Hindu communalist with links with the Hindu Mahasabha, RSS and V D Savarkar. As Sardar Patel as Deputy Prime Minister and Home Minister, had observed:

> It was a fanatical wing of the Hindu Mahasabha directly under Savarkar that [hatched] the conspiracy and saw it through.[4]

Patel had also expressed shock at the RSS distributing sweets after Gandhi ji's murder.

A lesson can be learnt from how our nationalist leaders, Gandhi ji and after him Nehru led from the front in dealing with this extreme arousal of communal hatred. Gandhi ji spent four months, November 1946 to March 1947 walking in the remote villages of Noakhali to contain the communal situation while the transfer of power from Britain, one of the biggest events of the 20th century, was being negotiated in New Delhi. He then went on to Calcutta and Delhi staking his life to quell the riots leading Lord Mountbatten to describe him as a 'one-man boundary force'. Gandhi ji's last fast onto death in Delhi, shortly before his assassination, was to stop the rioting in Delhi after independence and Partition.[5]

Nehru on his part (as head of the interim government) rushed to Bihar, and between 4 to 9 November 1946, along with virtually the entire top leadership of the Congress—Sardar Patel, Rajendra Prasad, Maulana Azad, Acharya Kripalani, Jayaprakash Narayan, Anugrah Narayan Sinha and many others toured the affected areas, determined to stop the violence immediately. Nehru put his own life at stake and declared immediately on reaching Bihar:

> I will stand in the way of Hindu-Muslim riots. Members of both the communities will have to tread over my dead body before they can strike at each other.[6]

On his Independence Day speech from the Ramparts of the Red Fort in Delhi on 15 August 1947 he made it clear that communal strife will not be tolerated and that India will be a secular state and not the mirror image of Muslim Pakistan, a Hindu state. Nehru declared:

> The first charge of the Government will be to establish and maintain peace and tranquillity in the land and to ruthlessly suppress communal strife... It is wrong to suggest that in this country there would be the rule of particular religion or sect. All who owe allegiance to the flag will enjoy equal rights of citizenship, irrespective of caste and creed.[7]

Barely had the communal situation come under control that Mahatma Gandhi was assassinated. Nehru was very clear that 'this assassination was not the act of just one individual or even a small group... behind him lay a widespread organisation' and he made it clear that the organisation he was referring to was the RSS.[8] In fact, he saw it as an effort to change the very nature of the Indian state by seizing power. In his letter to the Chief Ministers on 5 February 1948 he did not mince his words:

> It would appear that a deliberate *coup d'état* was planned

> involving the *killing of several persons* and the promotion of general disorder to enable the particular group concerned (RSS) *to seize power.* The conspiracy appears to have been a fairly widespread one, spreading to some of the states.[9]

It was a threat to the very 'Idea of India' as a secular country and Nehru was not about to let it succeed. With the full support of his Home Minister and Deputy Prime Minister Sardar Patel, he banned the RSS and put 25,000 of its activists in jail. Even when the ban on the RSS was lifted in July 1949, after it gave written assurances that henceforth it would function only as a cultural organisation and have nothing to do with politics, Nehru, remarkably presciently, warned the chief ministers of the fascist nature of RSS and the threat of their renewing their activities.[10]

Nehru's commitment to the secular ideal and his prescient understanding of the grave nature of the threat from the communal fascist forces is evident from the manner in which he converted the first general elections of 1951-52 into a virtual referendum on what was to be the nature of the Indian state. He made the fight against the communal political groups; his central objective and campaign was relentlessly for realising the secular vision of the Indian national movement. He travelled nearly 40,000 kilometres and addressed an estimated thirty-five million people or one-tenth of India's population. The result was that in a peaceful fair election held within years of the holocaust like situation and extreme arousal of communal frenzy, the communal parties, the Hindu Mahasabha, the newly formed Jana Sangh, and the Ram Rajya Parishad won between them only 10 Lok Sabha seats in a house of 489, and polled less than six per cent of the vote. It was a stunning achievement and a fitting tribute to the Indian national movement.

The communal threat was pushed back for decades to come. It was unfortunately not extinguished. Now that the communal forces threaten once again not only the nature of the Indian state but the very survival of the Indian nation. Mob lynching of Muslims have become common, open calls for genocide of Muslims are given with impunity and bulldozers are used to demolish Muslim homes and shops by the state.[11] So much so that The Punjab and Haryana High Court was constrained to take *suo motu* action intervening against the reported targeted bulldozing of properties of the Muslim minority saying the issue arises 'whether the buildings belonging to a particular community are being brought down under the guise of law and order problem and an exercise of *ethnic cleansing* is being *conducted by the state*.'[12]

Much needs to be learnt from how our tallest nationalist leaders challenged these forces head on, if we are to be able to save the secular Idea of India.

II

DEMOCRACY

Nehru's role in laying the foundations of a democratic structure in India was immense. We must look back at his effort at a time when the world is no longer accepting India as a full democracy. Our ranking in the Democracy Index has fallen to the 53rd position and we are being described as a 'partially free democracy', 'flawed democracy' or even an 'electoral autocracy'. The downgrading is a result of the growing state sponsored anti-minority feelings and strife, the decline in civil liberties, freedom of speech and curbs on the media and civil society movements.[13]

For Jawaharlal Nehru, democracy and civil liberties were of absolute values, which could not be compromised for any goal however laudable, be it planning, economic development or social justice. This impacted critically on how these other goals were sought to be achieved. 'I would not', declared Nehru, 'give up the democratic system *for anything*'.[14] In this he was reflecting faith in a non-negotiable core of the Indian national movement, democracy and civil liberties, best expressed by Mahatma Gandhi in his inimitable idiom:

> Civil liberty *consistent with the observance of non-violence*... is the foundation of freedom. *There is no room there for dilution or compromise.* It is the water of life. I have never heard of water being diluted.[15]

Nehru strongly believed that a country as diverse as India could be held together only by a non-violent, democratic way of life, and not by force or coercion. Only a democratic structure that gave space to various linguistic, religious, cultural, political, and socio-economic trends to express themselves could hold India together. Almost, as if anticipating the danger faced by the nation today, he said:

> This is too large a country with too many legitimate diversities to *permit any so-called 'strong man'* to trample over people and their ideas.[16]

Nehru also correctly saw that the heart of democracy lay in respecting difference of opinion, even if it be that of a minority. For him there was no democracy without an opposition. He said on 2 June 1950, before the first general elections:

> I am not afraid of the opposition in this country and I do not mind if opposition groups grow up on the basis of some theory, practice or constructive theme. I do not want India to be a country in which millions of people say "yes" to one man, *I want a strong opposition.*[17]

Now, unfortunately, '*Mukti*' (deliverance) from any opposition is declared as the goal; Congress *mukt*, 'Lutyens Delhi' *mukt*, Left-liberal *mukt, andolanjeevi/parjeevi* (agitationists/parasites) *mukt*, independently thinking universities, like JNU *mukt*, NGOs *mukt*, Amnesty International India *mukt*, Human Rights Organisations *mukt*, are some examples of what Bharat must be *mukt* of!

Part of this respect for the opposition for Nehru was civil liberties and the freedom of the press. As he put it in 1940:

> The freedom of the press does not consist in our permitting such things as we like to appear. Even a tyrant is agreeable to this kind of freedom. Civil liberty and freedom of press consist in our permitting what we do not like, in our putting up with criticism of ourselves . . . [18]

At the height of his popularity, Nehru had once famously published, with a pseudonym, a scathing critique of himself, saying that too much adulation if unchecked could produce 'Caesarism'.[19] Nehru's commitment to a free press was absolute and remained as strong when he was in government as it was when he was leading the struggle against the colonial state. No cartoonist had to go to jail in his times!

Nehru's respect for Parliament and parliamentary practices and codes of conduct, and particularly his respect for the opposition, was legendary. Stories of Nehru's praise for Atal Bihari Vajpayee's strong stands opposed to his own are reminiscent of Gandhi's attitude to opposition. He tried to institutionalise the cabinet system of government. Not only did he not usurp all powers to himself, he refused to give in to the tendency among many of his colleagues to leave important policy decisions to him. In his autobiography, C D Deshmukh, who was Finance Minister in Nehru's cabinet from 1950 to 1956, recorded that 'Nehru as head of the cabinet was gentle, considerate and democratic, never forcing a decision on his colleagues . . .'[20] Nehru's letters to the Chief Ministers, now published in five volumes, is a great illustration of how Nehru was trying to educate and propagate democratic values and practices among his political compatriots.

Nehru was very careful in trying to build democratic institutions with as little interference of the state as was possible whether it be the judiciary, bureaucracy and other institutions. This was particularly true of academic institutions. He said in December 1947:

> A university stands for humanism. For tolerance, for reason, for the adventure of ideas and the search for truth... If universities discharge their duty adequately, then it is well with the nation and the people. But if the temple of learning itself becomes a home of narrow bigotry and petty objectives, how, then, will a nation prosper or a people grow in stature?[21]

Some of the finest institutions were created in his time. Unfortunately, many of these institutions, like my university Jawaharlal Nehru University (JNU), struggle to survive the current assault on them where dissent is suppressed, often brutally. Students are beaten up by the police, arrested and put in jail for years and even denied bail, faculty is intimidated and efforts are made to alter syllabi to suit the governments biases. Almost all the institutions of democracy so carefully nurtured by are under threat. A return to Nehruvian practice in this regard is so essential today.

III

SOVEREIGNTY AND SELF RELIANCE

Nehru and the early Indian planners had correctly understood that political independence was of little value if it could not be used to acquire first economic and then intellectual independence. At independence, because of the nature of colonialism she was subjected to, India was almost completely dependent on the advanced world for capital goods and technology for making any investment which was necessary for the growth of the economy. It produced virtually no capital goods. In 1950, India met nearly 90 per cent of its needs of machines and *even machine tools* through imports. This meant that despite political independence, it was completely dependent on the advanced countries for achieving any economic growth through investment.

This was a *neo-colonial* type situation, which needed immediate remedy. And this is what the famous Nehru-Mahalonobis strategy tried to reverse by adopting a heavy industry or capital goods industry based industrialisation. During the first three Five Year plans (1951-65), industry in India grew at 7.1 per cent per annum. This was a far cry from the de-industrialisation process of the 19th century and the slow industrial growth between 1914-47. More important, 'the three-fold increase in aggregate index of industrial production between 1951 and 1969 was the result of a 70 per cent increase in consumer goods industries, a *quadrupling* of the intermediate goods production and a *ten-fold* increase in the output of capital goods'.[22] This shift was made possible by the imaginative use of the public sector moving into capital goods industries (A large number of them like HMT, BHEL, Hindustan Shipyard, Bharat Earth Movers, a number of steel plants, Heavy Engineering Corporation to name just a few came up in the Nehruvian period). This pattern of industrial development led to a *structural transformation* of the colonial legacy. From a situation where, to make any capital investment in India, virtually the entire equipment (90 per cent) had to be imported, the share of imported equipment in the total fixed investment in the form of equipment had come down to 43 per cent in 1960 and a mere 9 per cent in 1974, whereas the value of the fixed investment in India increased by about two and a half times over this period (1960-74).[23]

This was a major achievement as it considerably increased India's autonomy from the advanced countries in determining her own rate of capital accumulation or growth. It created the key condition for an independent foreign policy where India could lead about a hundred countries in the Non-Alignment Movement carving out a path independent of both the power blocs in the Cold-War era. In my understanding, no amount of diplomatic finesse could achieve and sustain the objective of non-alignment without the economic basis of relative autonomy having been created. It was this *un-structuring of the colonial structure* which was to later enable India to participate in the globalisation process with considerable advantage to itself.

It was not only translating self-reliance into Hindi and shouting *atma nirbharta* which was required but hard economic decisions which transformed the Indian economy inherited from the colonial rule.

However, maintenance of India's sovereignty and ability to stay non-aligned was possible only if India had food security. Indian agriculture had stagnated and even declined under the colonial rule and at independence India faced acute food shortage and famine conditions in many areas. 14 million tonnes of food had to be imported between 1946 and 1953. There could be no sovereignty if India was dependent on food aid and had had to go about with a 'begging bowl' for its very survival. Indian agriculture needed to be revolutionised and Nehru took up the task on a war footing. It is often wrongly alleged that Nehru ignored agriculture with his focus on industrialisation. He pushed through the extremely difficult task of land reforms *within a democratic framework*. The back of the nearly 200-year-old Zamindari system was broken within 10 years. Having achieved the institutional reforms in Agriculture through the land reforms Nehru laid the basis of the technological reforms leading to the 'Green Revolution', which made India food surplus in a remarkably short period.[24] As Daniel Thorner, one of the keenest observers of Indian agriculture since independence noted:

> It is sometimes said that the (initial) five-year plans neglected agriculture. This charge cannot be taken seriously. The facts are that in India's first twenty one years of independence more has been done to foster change in agriculture and more change has actually taken place than in the preceding two hundred years.[25]

Last but not the least Jawaharlal Nehru was acutely aware that true sovereignty could be achieved only if India became self-sufficient in science and technology, an area deliberately left barren in the colonial period. Nehru, therefore, made massive efforts to overcome this shortcoming. Right from the 1950s he set up a large number of institutions like the IITs, IIMs, AIIMS, the National Physical Laboratory, the National Chemical Laboratory, National Metallurgical laboratory, the Bhabha Atomic Research Centre (with the first atomic reactor going critical in 1956 and the first rocket tested from Thumba in 1963!) and numerous other institutions. An unprecedented increase occurred in the educational opportunities in science and technology in the universities and institutes. National expenditure on scientific research and development kept growing rapidly with each plan. For example, it increased from Rs 10 million in 1949 to Rs 4.5 billion in 1977. Over roughly the same period, the stock of India's scientific and technical manpower increased more than 12 times from 190 thousand to 2.32 million. A spectacular growth by any standards, a growth whose benefits India reaps today as the world moves towards a 'knowledge' society.[26] It is because Nehru anticipated the knowledge revolution that today is able to participate in this global phenomenon and nearly half of India's GDP is generated from the service sector which is based on the knowledge revolution. It is not despite Nehru but because of his farsightedness that India has reached where it has.

IV

PRO-POOR ORIENTATION

Nehru's success in keeping India on the democratic, civil libertarian path against considerable odds (while most other post-colonial countries faltered on this count), by itself ensured that the poor were not altogether left out of the development process or that their condition was not totally ignored. It is now well recognised that democracy is critical for the survival of the poor. It is democracy in India which has ensured that an inflationary path to growth, which hits the poor hardest, was never adopted. The trend rate of inflation in India since independence had not touched two digits for several decades. No government in India irrespective of their political ideology was able to ignore the political implications of uncontrolled inflation.

Also, it is democracy and civil liberties that ensured that no large-scale famine deaths could occur in India since independence, despite some extreme conditions created by climatic shocks, while more than 40 million died in famines in China in the late 1950s and 60s, which the world got to know decades later because of the absence of a free media. Amartya Sen has emphasised the role of civil liberties and a free press in preventing such mass man-made disasters. With more than 70,000 newspapers and about 700 satellite channels and with nearly 30 newspapers having a daily readership of more than a million it is not easy to keep famine conditions under cover in India.

While political democracy was understood by Nehru to be a necessary condition for people's empowerment, it was by no means taken to be sufficient. As he put it in 1952:

> If poverty and low standards continue then democracy, for all its fine institutions and ideals, ceases to be a liberating force. It must therefore aim continuously at the eradication of poverty... In other words, *political democracy is not enough.* It must develop into economic democracy also.[27]

Nehru took major steps in that direction. The land reforms, the Green Revolution, the Community Development Programme, the emergence of the public sector, the focus on education and health being a public responsibility, protecting of working class rights, the popularising of the socialist ideal were giant steps that greatly contributed towards an equitable society. Many of these steps are being reversed today with the privatisation of public sector enterprises and more shockingly handing over education and health to the rapacious private sector, rapid informalisation of labour with no trade union rights and making a mockery of the socialist ideal. The results are there for the world to see. India is witnessing obscene levels of inequality where we boast of our large number of billionaires while nearly half our children are malnourished. The world was shocked by the images of floating dead bodies in the river Ganga as the relatives of the deceased were too poor to do the last rites of their dear ones or that of thousands of migrant workers walking hundreds of miles to their villages at temperatures of 45 degrees centigrade, dragging their old and infirm and children to avoid starvation because of the sudden lockdown without adequate state support. We are slipping rapidly in the human development index and are today declared below sub-Saharan Africa in the hunger index!

Moreover, in these conditions the people's democratic right to mobilise protest which was guaranteed by our Constitution has been severely curtailed. Witness the manner in which the anti CAA movement and the farmers' protests were handled. Civil rights activists are branded as urban Naxals or as agitationists who are parasites (*andolanjeevi* and *parjeevi*).

There is a great need to return to the Nehruvian ideal here too.

V

SCIENTIFIC TEMPER

Nehru's focus on the need to develop a 'scientific temper' a term he coined in his *Discovery of India* which he wrote from a British prison in the 1940s, which the Constitution of India reiterated in article 51A laying down the fundamental duties of every citizen of India, is being made a mockery today.

The current Prime Minister, a few months after he assumed office, in October 2014, while inaugurating a new modern hospital in

Mumbai, mixing up mythology about Gods and Goddesses with history, told an audience which included India's top doctors, actors and business leaders, how in Ancient India we knew plastic surgery. He reportedly said, 'We worship Lord Ganesha. There must have been some plastic surgeon at that time who got an elephant's head on the body of a human being and began the practice of plastic surgery.[28] The Governor of Bengal, while inaugurating a Science and Engineering Fair, doing violence to both science and history, informs you that Arjuna, a major figure in the epic *Mahabharata*, had nuclear powered arrows.[29] The erstwhile RSS chief (*sarsangchalak*) K S Sudershan, an engineer by training, tells us about how Sage Bharadwaja and Raja Bhoj in times gone by not only 'described the construction of aeroplanes' but discussed 'details like what types of aeroplanes would fly at what height, what kind of problems they might encounter, how to overcome those problems, etc.'[30]

No wonder Corona is being fought by many with *Gobar*, *Gomutra*, *Thali*, *Tali*, *Ganga-snan* and unverified medicines made by a much favoured yogi!

In sum, Nehru's fantastic effort to raise India from what Tagore called the 'mud and filth' left behind by the British has now been replaced with the Indian people being pushed back into that same 'mud and filth' of ignorance, obscurantism, dis-empowerment, un-freedom and above all communal hatred.

NOTES

1 Krishnan, B Gopal in 'Kesari', Rashtriya Swayamsevak Sangh (RSS) mouthpiece in Kerala, 17 October 2014, see also https://indianexpress.com/article/india/india-others/godse-should-have-targeted-nehru-says-rss-mouthpiece/ retrieved on 17 August 2021

2 *Collected Works of Mahatma Gandhi*, Vol. 76, pp.389-90. The imagery used by Gandhiji for futile attempts to divide is very applicable to the current effort by the communal forces to constantly try to denigrate our freedom struggle by trying to point out differences between our national heroes like Gandhi, Nehru, Patel, Bose, Bhagat Singh, etc.

3 Quoted in Chandra, Bipan, Mukherjee, Mridula, Mukherjee, Aditya *India Since Independence,* New Delhi: Penguin, 2008, p.23

4 Das, Durga, *Sardar Patel's Correspondence, 1945-50,* Vol. VI, Ahmedabad: Navajivan Publishing House, 1973, p.56

5 For a detailed discussion on Gandhiji and Nehru during these critical years see Mukherjee, Mridula, 'Communal Threat and Secular Resistance: From Noakhali to Gujarat', *Presidential Address: Proceedings of the Indian History Congress,* Vol. 71, 2010-2011, 'Jawaharlal Nehru's Finest Hour? The Struggle for a Secular India', *Studies in People's History,* Vol. 1, No. 2, December 2014, 'Revisiting the Assassination of the Mahatma', *Marxist,* Vol. XXXV, No. 1, January-March 2019

6 Speech at Biharsharif, 4 November 1946, *Selected Works of Jawaharlal Nehru* (hereafter *SWJN*), Series 2, Vol. 1, 1984, p.57

7 *SWJN,* Series 2, Volume 4, p.2

8 *Jawaharlal Nehru: Letters to Chief Ministers* (hereafter *LCM,*) 5 February 1948, Vol. 1, p.56

9 Ibid., p.57

10 *LCM,* 20 July 1949 and 1 Aug 1949, Vol. 1, pp.412-13, 428

11 See for example 'In India, calls for Muslim Genocide Grow louder. Modi's silence is an endorsement', *The Washington Post,* 29 December 2021, *CNN,* 14 January 2022, https://edition.cnn.com/2022/01/14/asia/india-hindu-extremist-groups-intlhnkdst/index.html retrieved on 4 June 2022, *The New York Times,* 8 February 2022, https://www.nytimes.com/2022/02/08/world/asia/india-hate-speech-muslims.html retrieved on 4 June 2022, *The Economist,* 14 May 2022

12 *The Indian Express, The Hindu* and *The Times of India,* 8 August 2023, *The Telegraph,* 6 August 2023
https://www.livelaw.in/top stories/punjab-haryana-high-court-asks-on-nuh-demolition-drive-whether-buildings-belonging-to-particular-community-brought-down-as-exercise-of-ethnic-cleansing-234623,
retrieved on 9 August 2023, emphasis mine.

13 See https://www.bbc.com/news/world-asia-india-56393944 and
https://timesofindia.indiatimes.com/blogs/toi-edit-page/a-more-nuanced-democracy-there-is-no-need-for-it-to-be-only-what-the-west-says-it-must-be/
retrieved on 28 October 2021

14 Karanjia, R K, *The Philosophy of Mr. Nehru,* p.123 quoted in Chandra, Bipan 'Jawaharlal Nehru in Historical Perspective' in *The Writings of Bipan Chandra: The Making of Modern India from Marx to Gandhi,* New Delhi: Orient Blackswan, 2012, p.136, emphasis mine.

15 *Harijan,* 24 June 1939, *Collected Works of Mahatma Gandhi,* Vol. 69, p.356, quoted in *The Writings of Bipan Chandra,* op.cit., p.169, emphasis mine.

16 Karanjia, op.cit., p.139, emphasis mine.

17 Speech at Trivandrum, 2 June, 1950, in *The National Herald*, 3 June 1950; cited in Gopal, S, *Jawaharlal Nehru, A Biography,* Vol. 2, 1947-1956, p.68, emphasis mine.

18 *Selected Works of Jawaharlal Nehru,* (hereafter *SWJN*) New Delhi: Orient Blackswan, Vol. 11, p.367

19 *SWJN*, Vol. 8, pp.520-523

20 Deshmukh, C D, *The Course of my Life,* New Delhi: Orient Blackswan, 1974, p.205

21 *SWJN*, Second Series, Oxford University Press, Vol. 4, p.208

22 Vaidyanathan, A, 'The Indian Economy Since Independence (1947-70)', in Kumar, Dharma (ed.), *The Cambridge Economic History of India*, Vol. II, Delhi, 1983, p.961, emphasis mine.

23 See Mukherjee, Aditya, 'Planned Development in India 1947-65: The Nehruvian Legacy', in Akita, Shigeru (ed.), *South Asia in the 20th Century International Relations,* Tokyo, 2000. Also in Chandra, Bipan, Mukherjee, Mridula, Mukherjee, Aditya, *India Since Independence,* New Delhi: Penguin, 25th reprint, 2014 ch. 25. These figures are from an extremely persuasive piece by Vijay Kelkar, 'India and the World Economy: A Search for Self Reliance', Paper read at the Seminar on Jawaharlal Nehru and Planned Development, New Delhi, 1980, reprinted in *Economic and Political Weekly,* Vol 15, No 5/7, February 1980

24 See my chapters (29-33) on Land Reform and Green Revolution in Chandra, Bipan, Mukherjee, Mridula, Mukherjee, Aditya, *India Since Independence,* New Delhi: Penguin, 25th reprint, 2014

25 Thorner, Daniel, *The Shaping of Modern India*, New Delhi: Allied Publishers, 1980, p.245, addition in parenthesis mine.

26 See Mukherjee, Aditya, 'Indian Economy, 1947-65: The Nehruvian Legacy', in Chandra, Bipan, Mukherjee, Mridula, Mukherjee, Aditya, *India Since Independence*, op. cit.

27 *LCM*, 16 June 1952, Vol. 3, p18

28 https://www.theguardian.com/world/2014/oct/28/indian-prime-minister-genetic-science-existed-ancient-times retrieved on 19 August 2021

29 https://www.hindustantimes.com/india-news/arjuna-s-arrows-had-nuclear-power-chariots-flew-says-bengal-governor-dhankhar-draws-flak/story-M185xVdjIP8JbzTsSDRkOJ.html retrieved on 19 August 2021

30 See the RSS mouthpiece *Organiser*, 4 November 2001

Nationalism: Then and Now

S Irfan Habib

We are living in hyper nationalist times and this is the sole reason why we need to talk about nationalism now more than ever. We need to talk about it because it is part of our everyday social and political lives, our economics and we are so entrapped in the idea of it. Now, let us ask to ourselves, why is it so important? This question is going to form the base of this discussion.

For us Indians, the ideas of nation and nationalism are not really new. These have been part of our legacy. The ideas of India, of Indian nationalism, of the Indian nationhood itself are inheritances of our freedom struggle. Our ancestors have spent their lifetime in defining nationalism for us. Nationalism remained almost intrinsic to our growing up years even after Independence. But today, as the times are different, we probably don't need to be the kind of nationalists our ancestors were because nationalism was basically a tool for them to fight against the colonial oppressors. However, we do need to have a fresh look at how we can understand nationalism in present times and to do that we need to go back to our ancestors, the ones who fought for India's freedom; I will name them one by one—who thought about India better than us, who understood India better than us, who understood Indian society better than us.

We often see that there are names which do the rounds whenever the question of nationalism is brought up. These names are usually used by politicians in power. Subhas Chandra Bose, Bhagat Singh, Gandhi and Ambedkar and even Maulana Abul Kalam Azad are the names that one usually hears being brought up all the time. But merely naming them and beating about them around the bush would not yield anything. In order to understand the legacy that they have left behind for us, one has to understand what they stood for, what their ideals were and the idea of nation and nationalism they wanted to convey to us through their writings, statements, and political speeches. But in order to do so, we first need to understand that nationalism, actually, is not something which we created here in India. It is rather something that was imported from the 19th century Europe. Nationalism, as a tool to incite a feeling of oneness among the people of a country, was extensively made use of by countries like Germany, Italy, France, etc, as Europe was headed towards a crisis that eventually gave way to the world wars. There is no gainsaying that the ideas of nationalism and nationhood are outcomes of European experiences and these were passed on to us by the British. Here, I would take, for example, the testimony of Bal Gangadhar Tilak who is actually called the father of Indian nationhood and nationalism. Tilak wrote not once but several times that nationalism is not an Indian idea, that it has been imported from abroad and that we had to make use of the idea for our own struggle against colonial oppression. In fact, the idea that India was a nation for centuries does not hold any water. People like Lala Lajpat Rai, who wrote extensively on this, were in fact wrong in their premise because the idea of nation itself is a very modern one.

However, in India, a lot of public intellectuals have talked and written about it. For example, Tagore has extensively toyed with the idea of it, but we need to understand what exactly he was trying to say. Tagore never talked about a uniform political identity or national identity. Rather, he stressed on the importance of geographical identities, spiritual identity and such other forms of identities which will resonate different types of Indianness. From the late 19th century onwards, people like Tilak, Gopal Krishna Gokhale, Surendranath Banerjee, Mahadev Govind Ranade began thinking about nationalism in retrospect with the ideas of Indian nation and nationhood. All of them defined nationalism in their own way. Many of them used religion to define it. But their usage of religion was empathetic in the sense that they didn't use religion to exclude anybody, they used religion in a very positive manner. For example, Bipin Chandra Pal wrote about Medieval India and noted how it had been home to diverse people and diverse races that came to India. He observed how the Muslims, who preceded the British, in terms of coming to India, did not intervene in or challenge the cultural practices of Hinduism.

So, all those people who talk about perpetual bloodshed during the medieval centuries are actually wrong. They should, in fact, go back to the great nationalist leaders of India whom they espouse and venerate all the time and try to understand the message they wanted to give out by reading and understanding what they stood for. Not just politicians and leaders, even our great scientists like Prafulla Chandra Ray or Jagadish Chandra Bose for example, talked about India and the idea of the Indian nation and also of togetherness. Prafulla Chandra Ray wrote extensively on this issue and his autobiography (*Life and Experiences of a Bengali Chemist*, 1932, 1935) is full of references to medieval India. I am emphasising the medieval times, because it is an obsession we are living with today and we tend to define our idea of nationalism in the light of what happened in medieval India. An idea that is constantly peddled today is that medieval rulers, the Muslims in this case, destroyed us as a nation. But we have to understand how our scientists and intellectuals looked at this medieval past while they were defining the Indian nation or nationalism. We must also understand that nationalism cannot be defined by political leaders only. The opinions of public intellectuals, poets, scientists who have defined the lives of Indians in so many ways matter as much.

Unfortunately, all those who are trying to talk about Indian nationalism and nationhood are so far away from this India I am talking about today. We need to understand that the idea of India should be defined by what our great ancestors espoused it to be, what they wished the country to become as and when it became free from the colonial rule, and that it should never be defined by the cheap peddling of ideas which are not based on any historical truth, rather, on absolutely imaginary facts.

So, the present can never be underscored by imagining the past. The past should always be understood in terms of facts. But the opposite is done today and needless to say, it is a sort of vandalisation of history. We see history being peddled through WhatsApp. Today, a certain message is circulated among 2,000-3,000 people and that becomes a historical fact! For people like us, it is an immense task to actually undo that untruth. So, in the name of inciting nationalism, citizens of this country are being fed with untruth. We all need to question that, because if we let that continue, it will destroy us as a nation and as a society.

Now, going back to my postulate of understanding what our great leaders actually meant by nationalism, let us take the example of Subhash Chandra Bose. When we talk about him, we forget that Bose was not just only about the Indian National Army (INA) or Azad Hind Fauj. It was, in fact, his last-ditch battle against the British. To understand him wholly, it is imperative to see him in the light of what he was doing in the 1920s and in the 1930s. These two decades were the most formative phase of his life, politically and intellectually. He wrote extensively, mobilised the youth all over the country along with Jawaharlal Nehru, formed the Independence League and passed on the idea of Indian nationalism, of scientific temperament, scientific understanding, women's rights, etc. These are all, in fact, part of Subhash Chandra Bose's idea of nationalism. One just can't exclude these and concentrate only on how he led the INA in the face of extreme challenges. Bose once wrote that,

> Communalism will go only when the communal mentality goes. To destroy communalism is, therefore, the task of all those Indians—Muslims, Sikhs, Hindus, Christians etc. who have transcended all the communal outlook and have developed a genuine nationalist mentality.[1]

So, he is very clear in saying that a communalist can never be a nationalist! So, that is Subhash Chandra Bose for us.

We also talk of Ambedkar all the time. He generally kept away from talking about nationalism as such because his agenda was education and development of a particular section of people of our society. But he did discuss about nationalism in a book which he wrote on Pakistan and when he formed a Labour Party in Maharashtra in the 1930s. As Labour Party leader, he wrote a few things from which I quote,

> If nationalism means the worship of the ancient past—the discarding of everything that is not local in origin and colour—then Labour cannot accept nationalism as its creed. Labour cannot allow the living faith of the dead to become the dead faith of the living ('labour' here means the party which he formed).[2]

For Ambedkar nationalism was not a sacred creed, and he was not obsessed by nationalism. For him, nationalism was a tool which will bind people together not only on the basis of communities but also on the basis of class, poor and rich, all of them have to come together to formulate this nationalism.

Another name, which circulates very widely these days and is often used by the right-wing in their political programmes, is that of the iconic nationalist, Shaheed Bhagat Singh. Now, there is no disagreement that Bhagat Singh is a great martyr, but he has left behind something more than martyrdom. But treating Bhagat Singh solely as a martyr who gave his life on the altars of freedom struggle would be to undermine the values and ideals for which he stood. To understand him wholly, it is important that we know what was his vision of an independent India, what sort of nationalism he actually wanted to leave behind.

Let me digress here a bit to just talk about the importance of

1920s in our national struggle because the decade saw the first non-cooperation movement of Mahatma Gandhi, the birth of the Rashtriya Swayamsevak Sangh (RSS), the founding of the Communist Party of India, the flourishing of revolutionary ideology of Bhagat Singh and his associates in 1920s, the birth of Tabligi Jamaat, a Muslim communalist group. It was also a decade, which saw a huge labour movement in industrial areas. So, it was a decade which saw huge activity all over India and a lot of communalism as well because after the non-cooperation movement and the Khilafat movement, our nationalism somehow got divided along religious lines. Now, going back to Bhagat Singh, it must be noted that one of his cardinal beliefs was that there cannot be a nation unless people start thinking of India as one singular entity and that there cannot be any division on the basis of religion or caste. In 1928, Bhagat Singh wrote an article in which he vocally engaged against every sort of discrimination and injustice and pointed out that unless Indians grow out of their prejudices, it is futile to demand justice and equality from the British. He also wrote about the press and its responsibility of building a composite nationality. But unfortunately, today, the same press is actually dividing us. People often talk about his essay, 'Why I am an Atheist?' (1930), and I always say that it is not about any anger against God. It is more about emphasising on scientific temperament and rational thinking. He also wrote about leaders and leadership and emphasised that one cannot be a blind follower of any leader. Rather, one needs to introspect and judge a leader by his/her deeds and actions. We need to understand that these are the people who defined nationalism for us in 1920s and unfortunately we do not realise it.

We often talk about Sardar Vallabhbhai Patel but we hardly talk about what he wrote, what he spoke, what sort of India he wanted. I just want to quote one instance. In 1949, two years after the independence, he gave a speech about building a New India. He clearly stated about his disagreement with both the Left and the

Right and his vision of building an India which is socialist, which is on the Bolshevik lines. When it comes to the right-wing, they want 'Akhand Bharat' which is damaging the soul of India as we have already suffered a lot during the Partition. Pointing it to the right-wing, especially after the assassination of Mahatma Gandhi, Patel said they should start respecting the National Flag. Sardar Patel, as a home minister and as deputy prime minister, had to remind them that if they respect the National Flag, only then they could be nationalist; how can one be a nationalist without respecting the National Flag? We need to always remember and talk about what these great leaders of our country said and believed about the idea of India because nationalism is not an empty word or a political rhetoric. It is rather the legacy of our great leaders who churned this idea to leave with us a composite, indivisible, and integrated country. Mahatma Gandhi had once remarked that one can still be a nationalist without the influence of any external factor. But today, what people actually do is that they start defining nationalism vis-à-vis an enemy they deliberately try to figure out which is questionable in the light of how our great leaders wanted the idea of nationalism to function.

I could actually refer to Maulana Azad as well, because he was someone who was battling two communalisms, the Hindu and the Muslim, to defend his idea of composite nationalism. His idea of an indivisible composite nationalism was a challenge because he battled more than anybody else. In his presidential speeches, in 1923 and in 1940, in Ramgarh at the plenary session of the Indian National Congress, he noted that India belongs to everyone who lives here. Even though Hindus have been living here ever since eternity, Muslims too have spent more than 1,000 years and now they have a right like anybody else to claim India their home. He also wrote a long piece on Islam and Nationalism, where he defined nationalism in the light of Islam. He noted that building a composite nation is possible because the Prophet, in the 7th century formed the first nation in the Islamic world in Madina, by forming a collaboration of Jews and Muslims. If the Prophet can do it, can the Hindus and Muslims in India. Today, I say it with a lot of conviction that Maulana Azad was able to convince a large section of the Indian population, Muslims in particular, that composite nationalism is possible, living together is possible. Large number of Muslims decided to stay back in India because people like Maulana Azad, Hussain Ahmad Madni, Allah Baksh Soomro and so many others, whose names we don't even know, who were against Partition, convinced them that India is their home. In 1940, The Azad Muslim Conference moved against Partition. It was the same year when the All-India Muslim League decided to pass a resolution on Partition. More than one lakh Muslims gathered in Delhi under the leadership of Allah Baksh Soomro who decided and declared almost a battle against the Muslim League and their idea of Islamic nationalism and division of India on the lines of community, two nation theory, etc.

We need to remember always that our nationalism is not just an idea based on majoritarian nationalism. It was not just Hindu nationalism because if it were so, then Bhagat Singh, who was an atheist, would not have been a nationalist! So, there is more to nationalism than religion. These are, culture, language, and most importantly, the feeling of togetherness. We can understand these factors only when we go back to our leaders who defined nationalism for us. We must make sure that we don't want a divisive India. We don't want India to be divided along the lines of caste, community, or religion because this is not the vision that the leaders of the freedom struggle have left behind. We decided in 1947 to be a Democratic Secular country unlike Pakistan, which decided immediately, to be an Islamic nation. We rejected the idea of a religious nation in 1947 itself. There is no need to go back to that vision. Let us just look around at our neighbouring nation and ask ourselves—where they are and where are we? So, if we want to be like them, the mirror image of what they have become today, then the choice is before us and we can very well decide what sort of national identity we want and what exactly is progressive for us or what exactly is the foundational idea of India for us.

NOTES

1 Bose, Subhas Chandra, 'Towards Communal Unity', 24 February 1940, in *Forward Bloc: A Political Weekly,* 2 Vols, Kolkata: Lokmat Prakashani, 2008

2 Moon, Vasant (ed.), 'Labour And Nationalism' in *Dr. Babasaheb Ambedkar Writings and Speeches,* Vol. 10, Mumbai: Dr. Ambedkar Foundation, January 2014, p.60

Dalit, Adivasi, Caste & RTI

People's Right to Accountable Governance

Anjali Bhardwaj

We all remember the absolute mayhem of the second wave of COVID-19 in the country with people running around from one hospital to another looking for beds with oxygen and ventilators, and many people collapsing on the way. We also remember getting up every morning and hearing depressing news about hospital running out of oxygen and people losing their lives. When the Parliament was asking questions about the of number of deaths due to oxygen shortage, the response from the government was that they have no information about anyone dying due to lack of oxygen. This was not the only thing the government said. It had the same response when asked about the number of migrant workers who died while walking back to their villages during the lockdown. The government also said that it has no information regarding unemployment in the country and also no information is available on consumer expenditure index or the deaths of manual scavengers in the country. So essentially, whenever the government has been questioned about things that are inconvenient to respond, the general response has been that there is no information.

No information basically means no accountability. If I were to reimagine India, I would imagine a country where the state is accountable, where those in power are answerable to the people of the country. For that to happen, at least three things have to take place:

- The first, every person, the last person on the street has to be empowered to ask questions to those in power.
- The second is that, the ones who ask questions and raise dissenting voices, need to be able to do so without the fear of being crushed by violence and attacks unleashed against them.
- And finally, when people ask for answers, file complaints and expose wrong doings, corruption, human rights violation, there

must be systems and institutions that take actions and investigate the same to ensure that the grievances are addressed properly.

In 2005, a very powerful Right to Information law was brought in because of a strong people's movement. The movement involved citizens, people from across the country from slums in urban areas to villages and other remote areas of our country. People came together and asked for a strong legislation. The law has also been used vibrantly—more than 60 lakh people file RTI (Right to Information) applications every year in our country. It is the highest anywhere globally. They are asking for information for very basic rights like ration, pension, information about education of the children in government schools, medicines in hospitals to questioning the highest offices of the land like the Big-ticket corruption, the Adarsh Scam, Vyapam Scam, Rafale deal, etc.

People have asked the judges of the higher judiciary—the Supreme Court, the High Court about their assets and liabilities to see whether there is any judicial corruption. Information has been asked about the educational qualifications of our Prime Minister as well. In 2014, when the Bharatiya Janata Party (BJP) came to power on the plank of anti-corruption promising a more transparent accountable governance, the hope was that the one instrument that empowers people to be able to hold the government transparent and accountable, 'The Right to Information Act', would be fortified. But what we have seen in the last seven and half years is a systematic dismantling of the Right to Information regime in our country. We have seen how the governments have just put up their hands and said we just don't have data and stopped providing basic information.

Again, we have seen how the governments have brought in various schemes and systems with secrecy built into them. We all know that the fountainhead of corruption in our country has been political party funding. But instead of ensuring a greater transparency in political parties funding the government, the electoral bond scheme basically, opens the floodgates to anonymous, unlimited donations to political parties from people and organisations from within and also outside the country. This is dangerous because we know that in a democracy, political parties form the government eventually when they win. The political parties are obviously going to work for the benefit of those who fund them. So, there is a deep-interest in democracy for citizens to know who is funding which party. If I want to know whether the Ambanis, the Adanis, the Tatas, the Monsantos are funding any political party, I would want to be able to cast my vote in an informed manner. But what the electoral bonds scheme has done, that it has disempowered the citizens from knowing who is funding the political parties. So, we go in a sense blind-folded to vote in elections. We have had in last three years, since the electoral bond scheme was brought in, several states had elections, and we even had a general election, where the Bharatiya Janta Party, which had received more than 70% of the electoral bonds money so far, had won elections.

We were told that the PM Cares Fund has been set up to help people get through the COVID-19 crises during this disaster time, but nobody was being told how much money is coming into the PM Care Funds and from where or who is donating the money, where the money is going, etc. So, there is this whole secrecy, which is being practised by our government at the moment. When people want information, they are supposed to go to information commissions, that are supposed to function on behalf of the people. To make sure that the governments give information, direct them to disclose information, even it is inconvenient for them to give the information. But what we have seen is that instead of empowering these information commissioners, and allowing them and having a framework where they can function autonomously and independently, their independence has been undermined. First of all, not a single information commissioner has been appointed to the central information commission since 2014 without people going to courts. So, there are vacancies that come up in the information commission but no appointments are made and the posts lie vacant.

As a result, the number of pending cases keep going up and people have to keep waiting with their appeals and complaints and not get their right to information.

Again, the RTI law was amended very recently where the government changed the provision of the RTI law in which the salaries, the terms of reference and the time period for which appointments of information commissioners are made. So, essentially, the information commissioners are forever worried that if they have to direct information disclosure that the central government is not happy about, then their pensions, their salaries, terms of reference could be harmed. So, what we see is nothing but direct attack on people's Right to Information.

We need a situation, we need a country where there is free flow of information, where the governments are held accountable, where they maintain information, that information is disseminated to people. It is disseminated proactively by governments. Information that is in public interest, is not given in just technical forms not just online but in offline modes in local languages so that every citizen in the country can participate. Every citizen in the country can know that if there is a law passed in the Parliament what are the basis for which the law has been brought in, what is the basic structure of the law before hand, so that they may participate meaningfully. There can be pre-legislative consultation. We need a system where if the government don't share information they are held to account.

Again, if you look at what happens to those who question, in the state of Madhya Pradesh just outside Bhopal, few years ago there were extra-judicial killings, people asked questions and a senior Union Cabinet Minister went on record to say that there is a terrible culture that has set into the country—the culture of questioning. Now, this statement is highly problematic. In a democracy, people should have the right to question everything. We are being told that the culture of questioning is problematic and we have seen this permeates itself across the society where those who question, dissent and demand answers, are being attacked. There is violence against them; people are being killed for asking questions that are inconvenient. According to a recent update of National Campaign for People's Right to Information, more than 95 people have been killed in our country while 211 people have been harassed with 163 persons sustained physical assaults, simply for filing RTI applications and exposing corruption and human rights excesses. We know how people who are raising their voice and questioning unconstitutional acts are being targeted. There are false cases against them under the draconian laws like UAPA, NSA, etc, and they are labelled as anti-national or Urban Naxal. That is how the atmosphere of fear and intimidation is created against those who raise questions.

What we need is a safe space for people to openly question and participate, for people to assert themselves have the freedom of expression, freedom of speech and the freedom to ask. And that is only possible when there are governments that recognise that they have been elected by the citizens of our country to simply work on their behalf. They are willing to be transparent and there have to be mechanism and systems like the Whistleblower Protection Act, 1989 which protects people who ask questions. The Whistleblower Protection Law was passed in 2014, till date it has not been operationalised because the government has refused point-blank to make and promulgate rules of Whistleblower Protection Act. So, despite being the law is there on the statute book, it is absolutely useless for the people who are asking questions.

Finally, in order to be able to hold governments accountable, citizens need a system where they can go to where they can complain, raise questions and take their grievances and cases against the wrong doings of the government. We don't need a system where the government would constantly pat themselves on the back and say that they are not corrupt and that no wrong doing is happening but the systems and institutions that are supposed to do oversight and hold the government accountable, don't function. We need an affective grievance redressal mechanism by which the people who don't get the basic rights, file a complaint that doesn't just go into a black hole but is acted upon in a time bound manner so that problems are addressed and people get their basic rights and entitlements. We need an institution, which is independent and empowered to look into cases of corruption and human rights excesses. The Lokpal Law was brought in, but we know how appointments are being made to the Lokpal, Lokpal, the Enforcement Directorate (ED), Central Bureau of Investigation (CBI) etc. They are the people who are acolytes of the government and are brought in to raid peoples' homes who ask questions. Basically, they are brought in to act against citizens, who dissent and do not investigate and act against those who should actually be held accountable. So, we need a strong judiciary that acts on behalf of the people in our Democracy.

So, I imagine an India where there is real participatory democracy and our elected rulers are accountable to us, THE PEOPLE.

Re-imagining Status of Dalit Women in India: Reclaiming Dignity

Abirami Jotheeswaran

I would like to share the status of Dalit women in India, their overall socio-economic status and political representation, and violence Dalit women and girls are facing today. We have published a book, 'Dalit Women Rise to Justice: Status Report 2021' during the International Women's Day. It is an opportunity for me to share about the findings, what is the situation, what are the recommendations, and what is the way forward, we believe as part of All India Dalit Mahila Adhikar Manch (All India Dalit Women's Rights Forum).

CASTE AND PATRIARCHY

Dalit women constitute 10 crores of the population which equals to 8% of Indian population. Dalit women are continuously facing oppression on account of caste, class and gender. When we see oppression, we can't say that all women in India face the same kind of patriarchal problems. However, the manifestation of patriarchy for Dalit Women is not just based on their gender but also their caste. This social system is referred to as 'Brahmanical Patriarchy'. We see that the Brahmanical patriarchy is also responsible for creating a hierarchy and reinforcing power structure among women as Dalit Women and non-Dalit Women. As a result, solidarity between Dalit Women and non-Dalit Women is less due to caste identity than gender identity.

Because of 'Brahmanical Patriarchy', the Dalit women face more violence, oppression and exclusion based on their caste identity than their gender, as compared to non-Dalit women.

As a function of Brahmanical patriarchy, Dalit women have

historically faced a range of discrimination and violence based on caste-based occupation such as Devadasi system, bonded labour, manual scavenging, etc.

Devadasi is a religious practice of an Indian institution wherein girls are offered to Hindu deities. Being a Dalit is a kind of 'prerequisite' to become a Devadasi. It is a kind of temple prostitution, forced prostitution which still exists despite its abolition. As per the data of Anti-Slavery International, 2017, 93% of women who are involved in Devadasi system are Dalit women. It is clear that Dalit women, in large numbers, are in the Devadasi system which still exists. Similarly, when we look at the data of women involved in manual scavenging, about 95% to 98% are from Dalit communities.

In such kinds of occupation/employment, it is clear that Dalit women constitute a majority and due to this Brahmanical patriarchy, Dalit women are facing different forms of discrimination, oppression and exclusion in the community.

EDUCATION AMONG DALIT GIRLS

In terms of education, there is again discrimination; if we look at the enrolment rate of girls in primary schools, both Dalit and non-Dalit girls would account for 99%. But as we move to the secondary and higher secondary level, enrolment rate for Dalit girls drops to 72%, while non-Dalit girls' enrolment is still 94%. So the gender disparity started in secondary and higher secondary school education.

In higher education, the enrolment rate among the Dalit girls is as low as 15.6%, and non-Dalit is 34%. When the girls' enrolment started with 99% in primary education, the drop-out rate of the girl students is increasing in each and every stage as we move to higher education which is only 15.6% (NSSO 75th Round on Education, 2017).

Whenever we talk about reservation, all youth become agitated, they used to say Dalits have reservation. But there is disparity among

Dalits and non-Dalits in accessing higher education; we have seen that 15.6% for Dalit women and 34% for non-Dalit women. This data is only for enrolment, we don't know what is the final outcome, whether they were able to complete their education. There are numerous cases where we see caste based discrimination in higher education institution, because of which people have even committed suicide.

People say there is no practice of untouchability. I visited a primary government school in Rajasthan; a six-year-old boy was made to sit separately during the mid-day meal. It was very questionable why a six-year-old boy was sitting separately? When I tried to bring them together, take a group photo, the boy was not ready to come in the same group. And when I tried to bring the boy closer to the other classmates of the group he started moving in the other direction. So when we had an interaction we asked what is the thing? Why are you people not coming together? Some children in the group responded, pointing to the six-year-old boy that they are eating non-vegetarian food that we don't eat and their parents are involved in the occupation of cleaning filthy. So there are people who know where the person comes from, which hamlet he hails from, which community he belongs to, even in the primary schools in rural areas, this caste-based discrimination exists. Do you think through this reservation policy this six-year-old boy can continue till higher education bearing this kind of humiliation from the peer group?

So the people have to understand when we speak about reservations, they should know the ground reality and they should go and visit the places. Even though the constitutional provisions promote equality and provide for affirmative actions like reservations; it is striking that the Education Ministry recently stated that among 45 Central Universities, there are only 2 SC, ST vice-chancellors. Thereby, despite reservations at the decision-making positions, representations from the Dalit community are close to negligible.

EMPLOYMENT OF DALIT WOMEN

When it comes to employment women are less employed than men. There is a gender disparity between working women and men. When we compare the data with so-called 'upper caste' and Dalit women, we see that the Dalit women are employed more. So Dalit women's employment ratio is 24%, whereas the non-Dalit women's ratio of employment is 18%. So which are the areas where the women are employed, we have a ratio of 24:18, when we see self-employment—Dalit women are less; when it comes to services—Dalit women are less compared to the dominant caste women; when it comes to labourers, Dalit women are more. 41% of Dalit women are employed in the casual wage labour sector, while other caste women are only 13%. We can see triple times of Dalit women are largely employed in labour. So it clearly indicates that on the one hand the education among Dalit women is coming down and on the other Dalit women are more in casual labour employment (PLHF, 2017).

POLITICAL REPRESENTATION OF DALIT WOMEN

As we are all aware for more than 25 years, the Women Representation Bill has been pending in the Lok Sabha, which is giving voice to the reservation of women. People might think that SC/ST already has reservation in legislation, so what is their opinion, why do they want to support this kind of Women's Reservation Bill. Out of 543 members in Lok Sabha, there are only 78 women, out of these 78 only 12 are Dalit women. It is clear that there is a caste disparity between Dalit women and non-Dalit women in Lok Sabha. When there are 84 seats in Lok Sabha reserved for Dalits, among that we have only 12, contributing to only 17%. This is very minimal, there is no separate quota within the quota among the Dalit which should ideally be 50% for women and 50% for men. So one way or the other we are at the mercy of political parties. The thing that we are demanding through 33% reservation, will increase the number of Dalit women in the parliament from 12 to 28 MPs. We are demanding this to pass the reservation bill keeping Dalit women, SC/ST men, and other marginalised in mind for reservation. When giving 33% reservation for women, we acknowledge that within women's representation, there should be a representation of women across castes and tribes.

LAND OWNERSHIP OF DALIT WOMEN

As we all know that it is pride and prosperity to hold the land, there is a land distribution policy for SC and ST; it is clear, but what is the percentage of people who are holding land. Dalits hold only 11% of land with them in the entire population and 79% of the land is held by the dominant caste.

Dalit women holding land are very meagre. On the contrary, we see that 57% of Dalit women are agricultural labourers. The deplorable state is that though 57% of agriculture labourers are Dalit women, they are capable of holding land, cultivate and harvest and maintain, but still they are deprived of the ownership of land.

VIOLENCE AGAINST DALIT WOMEN AND GIRLS

Despite the constitutional safeguards and special legislations such as the Scheduled Castes & Scheduled Tribes (Prevention of Atrocities) Act, 1989, Dalit women continue to face multiple forms of caste and gender-based violence including sexual violence when they assert their human rights to access common resources and public places, access to education, claim land, right to wages, right to dignity, right to legal recourse, right to cultural freedom, right to choose a partner, instances of social mobility, political participation, etc.

The National Crime Record Bureau (NCRB) data records 15,855 incidents of violence against SC women and girls in 2021, which is a two-fold increase in incidents compared with NCRB 2020 (7,397 incidents).

In 2021, the NCRB reports that more than 10 Dalit women and minor girls are raped every day, but very few incidents come to surface. For instance, the gang rape and murder of a 19-year-old Dalit woman in Hathras, Uttar Pradesh, in September 2020 has highlighted the brutality against Dalit women where the district administration had forcibly cremated the body of the victim at midnight without her family's consent.

The crimes against Dalit minor girls alarmingly increased in 2021 as is evident by the registered number of cases of assault increased by 63.6% (336 incidents in 2020 and 550 incidents in 2021) and rape increased by 21.8% (1,055 incidents in 2020 and 1,285 incidents in 2021) under the SC/ST (POA) Act and the POCSO Act as compared to 2020.

Though the crimes against Dalit Women and Minor girls' cases are increasing, the conviction rate remains less than 25%, acquittal rates are more than 74%, and more than 96% of the cases are pending trial under the SC/ST (POA) Act. It clearly demonstrates the government's poor response in tackling atrocities against Dalit women and girls.

As a Dalit Women activist, I would like to reimagine India as a nation free from all forms of discrimination and violence, one that upholds the principles of the Constitution and provides equality, justice, and dignity to everyone—including Dalit women and women from all the marginalised groups.

I would like to reimagine India as a nation promoting gender equality, diversity, and social inclusion by incorporating human rights education in school curriculum from primary to higher education. Encouraging rational thoughts and scientific facts to shape the future generation as progressive and socially responsible citizens of India.

I would like to reimagine India, where free and compulsory education is offered to all children till the 12th grade, establishing upgraded infrastructure in all government residential schools ensuring holistic development (academics, sports, and extracurricular activities) with safety and security to all students with special focus on adolescent girls; thus ensuring greater enrolment of students from marginalised communities in the renounced colleges and universities for higher education. Despite the policy of affirmative action such as reservation, the reserved seats in premier educational institutions such as IITs, and IIMs go vacant, and deserving students from the Dalit community rarely get a chance to study in such institutions. Ultimately I would like to see adequate young Dalit women taking the lead in every space—be it academic, political, sports, business, law, and governance, playing an important role in the progress and development of this nation.

It is significant for us to have active Dalit women's leadership in all the fields including political representation in the Indian parliament with adequate/equal representation according to their population; thus Dalit women devising new policies and schemes for the development of this entire nation. Along with this, the private sector in India can make inclusive policies in their institutions/ companies to ensure the participation of Dalit women at the decision-making level.

We are re-imagining India where the discriminatory practices of work and division of labourers are abolished by practice. In this situation, the practice of undignified labour such as manual scavenging, bonded labour, etc will not exist in India. Modern equipment etc are invented to perform the menial job such as sewer cleaning. The people who were engaged in those occupations are rehabilitated as 'dignified' entrepreneurs. Access to basic services like health, food security, and housing to Dalit women, who want to leave manual scavenging, will ensure better work opportunities.

We would like to see Dalit women agriculture labourers be transformed into agriculture-holding communities and producing food grains and will be the beneficiaries of public policies that are designed for farmers. In this way, we would like to see India where Dalit women cultivate their own agricultural land and contribute to the growth of the Indian economy.

I would like to re-imagine India, where adequate measures are taken to implement all the legislation to prevent and combat violence against women and minor girls including women & minor girls from marginalised communities. The effective implementation of the SC/ST (Prevention of Atrocities) Act and the POCSO Act are central to preventing caste-based gender violence and delivering justice to the survivors. Adequate psychosocial measures are taken to heal the mental trauma of the survivors and encourage them to revive a new beginning.

We are reimagining India in respect of the socio-economic and political situation of Dalit women. Dr B R Ambedkar drafted the Constitution that changed modern India's perspective on socio-economic policies, and education in affirmative action. We are hopeful that the constitutional rights of the people will be protected without any discrimination based on their caste, class, and gender. Hence, every human being is treated equally with dignity and respect in India.

> 'Ours is a battle not for wealth; nor for power, ours is a battle for freedom; for reclamation of human personality.'
>
> —Dr B R Ambedkar

Caste and the Politics of Prejudice

Moggallan Bharti

Whenever we talk about the question of caste, we can't help but grapple with all the associated agenda that comes with it. So much of a discourse has been generated over the years, covering this subject, and that adds to our knowledge about how it functions. But, at the same time one may also feel that all the information, all the interpretation of the texts on caste and the available paths to address widespread social inequalities rooted in the system of caste is just too overwhelming. All the more so, in order to make sense of caste inequality today, especially since 2014 when widespread caste atrocities have taken place against the members of lower castes—constitutionally defined as Scheduled Caste (SC) and Scheduled Tribes (ST)—the dalits. When we see this widespread caste inequality, and the social exclusion it leads to, and the discrimination that it causes, we can't help but think together to re-examine our struggles, and devise a new path, a kind of a roadway ahead. Because, in the present times, instead of resolving the caste tension, instead of lessening of caste inequalities, what we see is an all the more sharpening of widespread social inequalities.

So, the first thing which I must underline, and we must understand that caste is not a singular subject, it is always plural. Ambedkar has explained this at great length in his paper *Castes in India*. That caste always works as a system and not on a standalone basis. In other words, caste has no meaning in itself, but it becomes functional in relation with other castes, and hence it is a caste system. The other problem with the common understanding on caste is that people try to project it as something happening in villages, and at a place which is socioeconomically backward. That's not true. Caste discrimination happens across the country, and among all the strata of society. I am not going into the detail about how caste system works—the four division of *varna vyavastha* and the *brahman, kshatriya, vaishya, shudra* and the Dalits being outcaste there. The point I am trying to drive here is that we must recognise and understand, that whenever we talk about social exclusion and discrimination rooted in the caste system, there is a large number of people who have an interest in strengthening this system.

Now, coming back to social inequality, we clearly see that it is widespread and along with social inequality, inequality based on class income, in terms of resources, is equally rampant. More often than not, class inequalities correspond with the caste inequalities. The question of social justice along with ways of providing some economic parity among the people are two central questions of politics—whether acknowledge or not—not just in India but in most other countries as well.

Now, in India social inequality acts as an umbrella term for every other inequality because you see if somebody who is born in SC or ST community is bound to be stricken by poverty much more than someone from non-SC/ST caste in some backward region of a country. The social identity or the social location of person determines his income category in India. Inequality in India then, which is social in nature, is very widespread and ubiquitous both in the social and in the economic sense of the term. We clearly see its impact in the political realm as it defines today's politics. Caste plays a foundational role predetermining socioeconomic inequalities in this country. But other than caste affecting and influencing the social and the political fabric, the same also affects our society at a much deeper psychological level. Despite having somewhat decent progressive policies, a progressive Constitution, and progressive social movements, the impact and the grip of caste has not diminished, and it seems that this big demon of caste is not going to go away any time soon, either.

So, the psychological impact of caste is basically that people at large believe in the system of castes. In other words, the ideology of caste is ingrained in the psyche of both the affected groups—among those who discriminate, as well as those who are discriminated against. And with the kind of ideological assertion and the general state of the Indian polity since 2014, such ideological attitude has taken a further boost. At present, the larger political firmament is led by Bhartiya Janata Party (BJP)—as the same party rules the national government—with the ideological support of Rashtriya Swayamsevak Sangh (RSS). The ideological atmosphere, thus enforced, is such that it has become all the more important to understand the nature of the psychological hold of a particular kind of politics which I call as politics of prejudice.

Prejudice in this context should be understood as the idea whereby people want to hold on to the privileges offered by the caste system. After all, the caste system is not all about lower castes and other socially backward castes. It also about socioeconomic privileges that it bestows to a tiny minority of upper castes. The resultant economic inequalities keep the huge population of the country on economic subsistence level, and sometimes even lower than that, while at the same time giving huge amounts of privilege, entitlement and power, both social and political, to a numerically smaller group who by accident of their upper caste birth status are, and have always been in the position to influence each and every policy, and the political outlook of the country at any given point of time. Professor Christophe Jaffrelot terms the continuation of politics of prejudice, especially since 2014 as the 'revolt of the upper caste'.

I would, however, say that this sense of ideological hegemony has always been there, much before 2014. The constitutional mechanism and the progressive policies that follows from the mandate of the Constitution has been able to dissolve the caste inequalities to some extent in the recent past. Although, that is now debatable in the light of new research and statistical evidences. The affirmative actions that followed from the constitutional safeguards for the marginalised has been able to uplift at least a sizeable section among the dalit-bahujans to a certain degree, seeing which people have now been saying that progress has been made in our society. But, this progress is set to be reversed with the rising atrocity of cases against the dalits and particularly dalit women. The growing attacks on reservation which again flows from the constitutional mandate is increasingly manifesting as reduced number of seats for SC/STs and OBCs in higher education. Reduction in fund allocations and in the special allocation plans for SCs and STs' empowerment, are all signs of an all-out apathy of the state for the marginalised in India. The way this politics of prejudice is growing and increasingly commanding the social support backed by wider political impunity —the data scientists and perhaps economists will tell you in a more commanding details—the stunted implementation of such schemes in higher education for the empowerment marginalised communities is going to go from bad to worse soon.

This politics of prejudice is happening through our families, our educational institutions, through the very society that we cohabit today. A French philosopher—Louis Althusser—had said that ideological state apparatus works in a nuanced manner to continue the ideology of the ruling classes. This apparatus plays a very crucial role in sustaining a particular social ideological belief system which helps the so called majority to be in power who are the beneficiaries of the kind of prejudiced politics enforced in the first place. This entrenched prejudice and its grip on our politics has seeped into our society, and has been enabled with state patronisation.

The political force of prejudice instigates and encourages people to discriminate against religious minorities, and against the members of dalit community. Essentially, a prejudiced mind will discriminate against any and every marginalised group except the members of their own—the community whose social belief feeds the politics of prejudice. How this ubiquitous ideological hate in India today has turn itself into an overwhelming political force is something we have to understand. We must understand the functioning mechanism of this politics of prejudice, if we want to counter it.

Now, one way to understand this politics of prejudice is to grasp and understand the ideology which has sustained it, and has always been there, and that ideology is the ideology of Brahmanism. To put it mildly, it is the ideology of the so-called majority, which is actually a wrong way to put the ongoing Hindutva tornado as the will of majority. This is definitely not the will of the majority. It's a big misconception. The actual vast majority of this country are the downtrodden working classes, marginalised communities, and other weaker sections. While the actual minority controls the maximum resources of this country and does everything in their power to maintain the caste system, in order to sustain their social status, to maintain their power and entitlement. This is definitely not majoritarianism. The so-called majority enjoys an ideological hegemony—an idea which is being endorsed and conceded to, by the vast section of the people who are in effect the victims of this ideology.

Actually that's how hegemony works—by the way of masses consenting to its sway. Hegemony can only succeed with the consent of people. Brahmanism as this hegemonic ideology enjoys mass approval. As the ideological force behind the politics of prejudice, brahmanism has massive presence everywhere in this country. How is that, that this cultural hegemony has taken roots with such widespread presence, and how does this affect our everyday lives, and *ipso facto* influences everyday politics is something which requires our collective attention and deliberation. One important thing must be kept in mind, that the dominance of the politics of prejudice—which Christophe Jaffrelot describes as the revolt of upper castes—has been completely frustrated by the upward mobility of dalits enabled by the politics of social justice and mandatory constitutional reservation of seats in public education and state employment. The upward mobility of OBCs—thanks to the Mandal Commission recommendations of reservation of seats in state employment in 1990s, and reservation of seats in public funded institutions of higher education in 2006—has also further triggered politics of prejudice. All this has somehow made upper caste extremely anxious over the years, and their social and political clout under threat from the growing political clout of the marginalised. They have been successful in politicising their caste prejudice and able to mobilise their hate against the marginalised into a political force and the result is what we see today.

The upshot of this growing political manifestation of social prejudices is what we witness in the form of increasing assault on the underprivileged classes, especially with sexual assault on dalit women—the gang rape and eventual death of a dalit woman in Hathras is the most recent such act. In fact, today's newspapers talk about the families living in that village are very fearful about the security of their lives and property. Asking for justice seems to be a far cry, as it doesn't appear to be accessible to the aggrieved family. Despite the police and judicial interventions, and despite people's protest and continuous press attention to the criminal case, justice is nowhere to be seen because the ideology of brahmanism pushed through the politics of prejudice is so entrenched that the whole incident has been normalised and seen as a routine crime, and not what it is actually about, and that being as the caste violence. How to counter this hopelessness, how to win over the people to see this madness, how to make semblance of things so that the politics of prejudice could be arrested, and be countered. In the next part we will see the possible ways to counter this politics of prejudices.

Resultant impact of the politics of prejudice has led to the concerted attacks on our educational institutions. What we saw in Jamia Millia Islamia in the year 2019 in the context of anti-CAA, and anti-NRC protests, whereby students were demonised and brutalised by the Delhi police. In the similar vein, in early 2020, violence occurred with the students and student leaders of Jawaharlal Nehru University (JNU). Much before this, how the student leaders from JNU were arrested on the charges of sedition, are all examples of the growing hold of a particular kind of politics which detests democratic dissent and is determined to build a country seen through the dominance of brahmanism. This attack on the sense of security of dalits, of religious minorities and different marginalised sections of the country—this all has been the ideological agenda of the politics of prejudice informed by brahmanism. How do we counter this politics of prejudice? In other words, how do we counter brahmanism, and counter we must.

One way of course has been to fight for the defence of what the forefathers of India's struggle for independence came up with—a progressive and inclusive Constitution. We must come together to defend this robust and inclusive framework for the governing this diverse country. By invoking the Constitution and the promise of politics inherent therein—promise of building a secular and democratic republic committed to equal opportunities for the marginalised—we will gradually be able to bring people out from the entrenched unequal social relations. The idea of such conceived a constitutional democracy like our modern republic, accommodative to politics of self-respect, of dignity of humans, of tolerating each other differences is of paramount importance today.

Despite the constitutional safeguards, the idea of achieving inclusivity in politics stands completely jeopardised today at the hands of prejudicial politics. The larger mandate and objective of our Constitution is under great threat today. Because for all this to work, one requires other's recognition of all the different ways of living in India; we all want to be respected and our civic agency acknowledged—traits crucial for the success of any democracy let alone a diverse country like us. This liberal frame is very important. It is the precondition for the politics to evolve further. For the politics to evolve to a point where it might upset the social and the material base of the political manifestations of prejudice today.

Largely, we must understand the nature of prejudice, and how it influences people's social behaviour. We must understand that when the prejudice is politically mobilised, the counter to that politics must also be mobilised. In other words, it's the people's collective effort, mobilised through social movement that has the essential material base to counter the ideology of hate and violence. There are no short cuts. We need an intense ideological struggle, where the progressive political forces, progressive individuals, and others have to come together for a common minimum programme wherein we must come to an agreement that certain values—enshrined in the Constitution—are non-negotiables. keeping the political differences aside, we must come together to forge such a 'non-negotiable' agenda. In order to achieve such a platform, the progressive political sections should come out in big number. We must come in defence of our Constitution for it's the precondition for a promising future political world to emerge. In the times where almost every institution has been squeezed, arm-twisted, and been hoodwinked to serve the interests of domineering politics of prejudice, we need to be prepared for protracted political struggle.

The role of civil society and progressive individuals is extremely crucial to achieve the objective of such a platform in defence of 'non-negotiables'. Moreover, this is not anything new. There have been innumerable examples of such initiatives from organisations and individuals in this country. For instance in south India and parts of Maharashtra where people like Narendra Dabholkar and others have been part of *Andhashraddha Nirmulan Andolon* (anti-superstition movements), which has played a big role in social and political awakening. Erode Venkatappa Ramasamy, revered as Periyar and his social and political contributions have been immense—the dividend of which can be seen in and as Dravidian politics of Tamil Nadu today. Such intense ideological struggle are lacking in the northern parts of the country. Consequences are manifested in the social prejudices becoming normalised in everyday politics. Anti-caste social movements is one way to counter social tensions emanating from deep seated social prejudice. That latter can only be countered to some extent if we mobilise ourselves ideologically, to combat social prejudices where it emanates from.

One of the important elements of the politics necessary to counter the politics of prejudice ought to be that there should not be any compromise in countering brahmanism. Given the reach and grip of brahmanism, there needs to be some political formulation to that end, where there is lot to learn from the ideological arsenal of the Ambedkarite movements. Drawing on Ambedkar's teachings and philosophy, dalit politics today, seemingly, appears to be losing the ideological grip on the alternative to the politics of prejudice—reasons for which we need not to go in now—however, its primary motive or ideological objective to achieve social justice is of utmost importance for defeating the politics of prejudice. At the same time, we must keep in mind that the politics of representation alone—one of the central thrust of Dalit politics—will not resolve the problems emanating from caste prejudices; political representation can certainly give us a significant voice in political spaces, but representation by itself it is not going to counter or diminish the overreach of the brahmanism.

One must come back to the politics of social justice—how we are going to achieve social justice is, is by bringing together common people who believe in common goals and common objectives; how do we try to create a common platform and start from the basics all over again; how do we challenge the politics of prejudice at grassroots where it controls people's psychology—these are some of the issues we should think on.

The necessary politics to counter politics of prejudice as mentioned before is there in the writings of Jyotiba Phule, Periyar, and Ambedkar, and the recent history proves that it has a tremendous guiding force to mobilise against prejudice. Now, in this re-imagination of Indian politics—prioritising politics of social justice—re-alignment of political forces is of utmost necessity to counter the huge ideological assault which we are facing today. We need to re-imagine our roles, especially those of the intellectuals who are not just from the universities spaces alone. There is a huge presence of anti-caste intellectuals in regional centres, in the mofussil towns, who have an important role to play today. In fact, students, intellectuals, activists, all have to come together to work out, to reframe, to rethink, and re-imagine this politics which could sustain not only our modern aspirations but could also see and work towards making society of equals.

In the last 70 years or so, the battle which we have won, the civic values that we have been able to instil to make this country a society that confers dignity to every citizen—at least in principle, if not in practice—are going to go astray, if not already, if we don't come together immediately in defence of India's Constitution. Sometime I really think, I talk to my colleagues, I talk to fellow friends that whatever differences Ambedkar, Gandhi and Nehru had among themselves in 1940s and 1950s, they have had put those aside and had come together to build the foundations of this beautiful country. But seeing the political reality today, it all seems that we are back to square one. We are inching towards a more archaic, much glorified 'Hindutva' system where only the caste Hindus can enjoy their privileges, power, and entitlements at the cost of the social lives of marginalised groups like dalits, adivasis, and religious minorities. This cannot happen in a democratic country.

For us, the battle to defeat this politics of prejudice is basically the battle to reclaim the Constitution. One thing that is certain is that, that in order to defeat this politics of prejudice, we don't have any option but to come together. A lot many important achievements are at stake here, but the central stake is the Constitution of this country. We cannot let that be completely trampled by the obscurantist right wing led by RSS-BJP, while we sit and don't do anything.

REFERENCE

Jaffrelot, Christophe, *India's Silent Revolution: The Rise of the Lower Castes in North India,* Columbia University Press, 2003

Rights: Minority, Children & Women

Why Should We Care for the Rights of Minorities?

Tehmina Arora

The Constitution of India has a comprehensive framework to protect the rights of individuals. This includes the Right to Equality, Freedom of Speech and Expression, Freedom of Movement, Freedom to Form Association, Freedom of Conscience, Right to Life, Right to Practise and Profess the Religion of One's Choice.

Also included in this framework are Minority Rights—the rights of religious minorities, linguistic minorities and other vulnerable sections of society, such as Dalits, Tribals, women and children. These rights include the right to establish and maintain educational institutions and the right not to be discriminated against in institutions set up by the State. Now, one can ask, 'Why should Minorities have separate rights?' Does that not mean that they are being separated from a collective national identity?

This is a valid question and not a new one by any stretch of the imagination. It existed even at the time of framing of the Constitution of India, and it is valid for us to reflect on these for that I would like to give you three points to consider:

'WHY MINORITIES NEED SPECIAL PROTECTION?'

The first is, by establishing the rights of minorities, we recognise that in society there are groups that are different from us, groups that are 'the other' and because of their 'otherness' and their distinct identity, they become more vulnerable, and this is the experience of minorities across the globe. You will find that minorities are frequently targeted and scapegoated. There are frequent attacks and often physical violence perpetrated on them. This is not new to India or unique to India, but instead, there are several minority groups across the globe, in fact, even in South Asia, you will find groups that are majority in one country, are a minority in another country and are frequently attacked because of their identity. This often leads to violence as well as a denial of their basic existence sometimes, a denial of their culture, their identity and even denying them basic rights to rent a house. Even in cities like Delhi, minorities suffer from structural discrimination. For example, during the COVID-19 pandemic—there were several media reports on Muslim groups being targeted for spreading the Coronavirus. They were frequently scapegoated and held responsible, resulting in several attacks against minorities.

The Centre for Study of Society and Secularism, a documentation centre, recorded 10 incidents where communal riots took place in 2020, which claimed more than 59 lives.[1] There were several instances of murders, lynching and physical assaults that took place during this time and similar attacks took place against the tiny Christian community. Christian Human Rights groups recorded over 3,700 incidents of violence in the period 2013-2023,[2] where Christians were physically assaulted and wrongly arrested on allegations of Religious Conversions. Democracies are often vulnerable to the tyranny of the majority, a situation in which the majority rule can be oppressive, it can completely disregard the needs and wants of the members of the minority community.

The second point is that we recognise that human nature and institutions are prone to abuses and all of us need checks and balances. There have been large stretches of Indian History where different communities have peacefully coexisted, they have been tolerated, allowed even to flourish, but this has not always been a matter of right, but rather at the will and fancies of the Person in Charge, the ruler of the day, and when that authority changes, we find a change in which religious minorities get treated, which means that the policy was a mere choice and not a matter of right.

To give you an example, the way the Constitution of India was framed, the Rights and the Protections that were given for the freedom of conscience, the Right to Practise and Profess the Religion of One's Choice, if one looks at the debates of the Constituent Assembly at the time, significant emphasis is given on the need to protect the need to choose the religion of choice and practise the religion of one's choice and yet despite those protections, despite Article 25 of the Constitution of India saying that we have the Freedom of Conscience, the Right to Practise, Profess and even Propagate the Religions of One's Choice, we have now in 9 states of India, laws that regulate how religious conversions take place. The Anti-Conversion Laws, as they are often commonly called, require that if there is a religious conversion, you must go and inform the District Authority, the District Authority will then investigate, whether the conversion is by force, fraud and allurement. People may say, 'What is the problem if a conversion is taking place by force, fraud or allurement, it should be checked', I would agree with you, accept the words 'force, fraud and allurement' are so vaguely defined in these laws that anything could be included in them.

There have been several instances where people have distributed blankets around during the wintertime and because of that they have been accused of converting people, where people have been running schools and they have been accused of converting people, there have been examples of people getting married and sadly under this new law, even marriages are being seen as an inducement of force to convert. And we have frequently seen media reports of people being arrested, and wrongly accused under these acts. This is such a departure from what we see as what the Constitution provides and how these laws now regulate a religious practice or profession of one's faith. Most recently, the Gujarat High Court held that the Gujarat Freedom of Religion Act should be stayed even as the cases decided before the High Court there. We have also had the Himachal Pradesh High Court saying that provisions where somebody must go and declare to the Magistrate when they are converting, who will be attending the conversion ceremony and why they are converting, those provisions should be stayed. Nobody should be required to give the State information like this. The High Court held that the State had no business in monitoring a person's religious aspirations. And these are the checks and balances we require in all society. The rights of vulnerable minorities must be articulated and protected and should not be left to the whims and fancies of those in power. Because all of us, sadly, require checks and balances.

Another reason we should be thinking about why minority rights should be protected is a quote by Dr Martin Luther King Jr, the civil rights activist in the US. He said, 'It may be true that the law cannot change the heart, but it can restrain the heartless. It may be true that a law cannot make a man love me, but it can keep him from lynching me.'[3] We all require laws and boundaries to respond to the 'other'. This is so desperately needed in our society, where a culture of impunity is reigning, where people can attack religious minorities, Dalits, women and Tribals, yet face no consequences. We need good, strong legislation to keep these things in check.

But sadly, laws are not enough, and Dr Ambedkar, who was the chairperson of the Constituent Assembly's Drafting Committee, stressed in his speech that '... the Principles of Liberty, Equality and Fraternity are not to be treated as separate items in a trinity; they form a union',[4] he says. In a sense, to divorce one from another will defeat the very purpose of Democracy. Liberty cannot be divorced from Equality, Equality cannot be divorced from Liberty, nor can Liberty and Equality be divorced from Fraternity. Without Equality, Liberty would produce the Supremacy of the few over the other. Equality without Liberty would kill individual initiative. Without Fraternity, Liberty would produce Supremacy of the few over the many. Without Fraternity, Liberty and Equality could not become the natural course of things, it would require a constable to enforce them. This fraternity that Dr Ambedkar described is the third crucial part of why we need to protect minority rights. Fraternity helps us to develop a sense of brotherhood among all Indians. It is Indians being seen as one group. It is the principle that Dr Ambedkar says that brings solidarity to social life.

This brings us to our third point. By recognising minority rights, we recognise that something more significant binds us together despite our differences.

For Ambedkar, this fraternity means a sense of common brotherhood of all Indians. If Indians are to be seen as one person or one people group, fraternity is required. It is this principle that brings solidarity and unity in social life. But fraternity does not mean absorption into a whole, but rather it is the respect for the other based on principles of common brotherhood and dignity of each person. Fraternity must undergird all human relationships for freedom, justice and equality to truly flourish.

The Constitution of India in the Hindi language uses the term '*bandhuta*' for fraternity. *Bandhuta* draws on this powerful concept of being bound together, united together, and knitted together; it is a powerful vision of the citizens of India coming together, joining hands for the sake of the country.

India is a salad bowl and not a melting pot, where each element loses its distinct identity; we are to preserve each other's distinct identity and flourish in that. Reverend Jerome D'Souza, also a member of the Constituent Assembly, had argued that a certain degree of homogeneity is required; however, absorption in the sense of cultural, religious, or any other absorption is something against which we must be guarded. The strength of this land will be based upon the strength of its members of different communities, and they will not achieve their full strength unless they hold themselves to convictions and ideals that are their very own. Cultural Autonomy, for which he pleaded and which has been promised so far, is not inconsistent with national strength; even though they sometimes appear to be opposed to national unity, it's consistent with it, D'Souza argued. And this is why it is crucial for us as a nation to come together.

In an insightful study by Dr Brian Grim, Dr Greg Clarke and Robert Snyder, global research shows that 'countries with lower level of religious hostilities and Government Restrictions on religion ranked higher in primary education, health, technical training, technological readiness, innovation, communications, transport and infrastructure, market efficiency, business sophistication and the list goes on and on. Religious Freedom, he would argue, would also contribute to overall peace and stability and help lower corruption.'[5]

Research suggests that as social and religious conflicts grow, the development of a nation is gravely impacted. Frequent sectarian violence, we know, has injured the Indian Economy. According to various media reports, as social tensions have risen in India, we have lost our attractiveness to global investors. Leading asset managers would point to the change in policy, the rise in sectarian violence and instability as critical drivers for restricting foreign investment in India.

We can ill afford this in the wake of the COVID-19 pandemic. Our nation is suffering on many fronts, especially on the economic front, and as sectarian violence increases, this will continue to impact our economic growth.

If we want to emerge stronger from this, we must learn to work together. We need to be able to stand up for the rights of religious minorities, linguistic minorities, and other vulnerable sections of society. We need to come together, not only because it makes sense for us as a nation and is good for us as a nation, but it also makes economic sense. We literally cannot afford it, and I hope that even as we dream about a nation where we will be able to find ways to work together, that has religious communities who even speak out for each other, stand up for each other, they will call out violence that is happening in the name of our religion. We will speak up for those who are different from us, and if India wants to emerge in a financially stronger position in the post-pandemic economy, we need to think about ways we will work together. The makers of the Constitution of India saw India's religious diversity as a strength and an integral part of India's ethos.

Addressing the Constituent Assembly, Dr S Radhakrishnan, then a member of the Constituent Assembly and later President of India, noted, 'India is a symphony, where there are, as an in an orchestra, differing instruments, each with its particular sonority, each with its special sound, all combining to interpret one particular score.'[6] It is this combination that this country has stood for.

NOTES

1 https://csss-isla.com/secular-perspective/communal-riots-in-2020-low-numbers-only-a-deception/

2 Sen, Jahnavi, 'Data: Rise in Attacks on Christians in India, Up Four Times in 11 Years (2012-2022)', *The Wire* (9 September 2023), retrieved from https://thewire.in/communalism/data-rise-in-attacks-on-christians-in-india-up-four-times-in-11-years-2012-2022

3 Speech on receipt of the Honorary Doctorate in Civil Law at University of Newcastle upon Tyne, UK on 13 November 1967

4 B R Ambedkar's speech introducing the Draft Constitution in the Constituent Assembly on 4 November 1948

5 They ranked worse in market size and macroeconomic environment. Grim, Brian J, Clark, Greg & Edward Snyder, Robert, 'Is Religious Freedom Good for Business? A Conceptual and Empirical Analysis', *Interdisciplinary Journal of Research on Religion,* No. 10, 2014

6 Constituent Assembly Debates, Wednesday, 11 December 1946

Reimagining India for Children[1]

Enakshi Ganguly

'There can be no keener revelation of a society's soul than the way in which it treats its children', that's what Nelson Mandela said (8 May 1995) to us. I would add to this—the situation of children in a society, in a country, or in a nation whatever you call it, is like a dip-stick, it's like a thermometer, it tells what ails it or what is good in it.

My father passed away on 7 March 2023. On 22 June 2023 he would have been 96. As a teenager he had been involved in the freedom movement—ferrying messages, helping organise marches and meetings.

When India became independent on 15 August 1947, as the Office Secretary of the Sub-Divisional Congress Committee, he helped arrange the celebratory public meeting in his then little town of Alipurduar (West Bengal) and was invited as the first speaker. He writes in his memoir, 'I still remember I had said spontaneously—although we have got independence no doubt, but its only political independence. We have a long way to go. We are still not economically free. We have to now get real freedom through our own efforts . . . I do not know how many in the audience understood this. I was 20 years old.'[2] Indeed, how many would have known how prophetic was the voice of this 20-year-old?

Like many others in his times, my father, had dreams for an 'independent and free' India. Born in Dhaka, he was also a child of Partition. With him gone, we lost yet another person from that era. But does that mean that we have also lost the 'spirit' of freedom that he and his generation believed in.

There have been some important developments in these seven and a half decades. There are plenty of laws, policies, plans, and schemes set up to protect children and their rights. The Eleventh Five Year Plan, for the first time, even had a separate chapter with Child Rights (Chapter titled—Women's Agency and Child Rights). Child budgeting has been adopted nationally and in several states. Almost every child is now enrolled in school, including more girls. Many more children are immunised, there is greater reporting of violence against children,[3] the silence and stigma around child sexual violence is breaking down, and incidences of child marriage have[4] decreased.

At the same time, while some old challenges that have confronted children remain, others have intensified, and new ones have emerged.

Inequities persist due to social norms, caste, religion, gender identity, disabilities, region, or ethnicity. 21st century has thrown up diverse challenges for children in the form of the market and the internet, etc. And although these are global challenges in a globalised world, our children are not untouched.

We have seen better enrolment of children in schools, yet retention rates are still not optimal. Elementary education is now a fundamental right for children between 6 and 14 years. But children still feel compelled to drop out of school—rather find themselves 'ejected' out. Fourteen years and elementary school means children find it hard to continue up to secondary levels or beyond—thereby lack even the most basic qualification for many technical jobs.

Those out of school disproportionately include girls, children living in rural areas, those from migrant and minority communities (including linguistic minorities), street and homeless children, those living in slums, working children and children with disabilities.[5]

There continues to be a rural-urban divide, many children are growing up in unplanned and poor living conditions in under-resourced habitations with limited or no access to the most basic services. So, children are on the move within the country, across the region and beyond. These are children who are on their own or with their families. This too has its own consequences, especially in a world in which ethnic and religious tensions are on the rise and forced evictions and displacement remain constant.

According to Housing and Land Rights Network's (HLRN) *Forced Evictions in India*[6] released in 2022, government authorities at both the central and state levels demolished over 36,480 homes, thereby evicting over 207,100 people from their homes across urban and rural India. Over 4 million people live in homelessness and at least 75 million people live in 'informal settlements' in urban areas across India, without access to essential services, including water and sanitation. A large majority of the rural population also lives in inadequate housing, without access to basic needs. The grave housing crisis in the country is further compounded by the state's unending practice of home demolition and forced eviction of marginalised and vulnerable persons in both rural and urban areas. When entire families are in shock and trauma, how can children be spared? In an earlier report of 2018 by HLRN, it had documented the increased vulnerability of children to abuse and that they had to drop out of school. For example, when families were evicted for the restoration of Korattur Lake in Chennai, traumatised by the shock of the eviction, a woman attempted self-immolation with her two young children, but was rescued in time.

Forced migration, human smuggling and trafficking, abuse and exploitation remain realities. There is increasing violence based on religion and ethnicity. Low female sex ratio remains a reason for trafficking of girls or early marriage—some as young as 10 years.[7] As per the data presented by the National Crime Records Bureau, 2,834, 2,914 and 2,222 children were trafficked in 2018, 2019 and 2020, respectively. Over 4,700 people were trafficked in 2020, of which 1,377 were minor boys, and 845 were minor girls.[8]

The skewed sex ratio remains a matter of concern despite years of programmes targeting the girl child—the latest *avatar* being 'Beti Bachao Beti Padhao'. As per the Census, 2011, the child sex ratio (0-6 years) has shown a decline from 927 females per thousand males in 2001 to 919 females per thousand males in 2011.

India ranks 107th out of the 121 countries with sufficient data to calculate 2022 Global Hunger Index (GHI) scores in the 2022.[9] With a score of 29.1, India has a level of hunger that is serious.[10] India still has one of the worst rates of child malnutrition in the world, and home to the highest number of child labour despite promise of economic growth.

Children are hungry despite increase in food production. Infant mortality rates may have come down, but access to healthcare is unaffordable in the wake of increasing privatisation of services. Children are among 25 per cent of the population that is multi-dimensionally poor[11]—a larger proportion of which is female. About 32.75% of the population in rural areas and 8.81% of the population in urban areas have been identified as multi-dimensionally poor, as per the National Multidimensional Poverty Index (MPI) 2021 Report.

Internet based communications and social media have created a completely new world. They offer innumerable possibilities, but have also brought hitherto unknown forms of exploitation. Young people find themselves increasingly lost in the new market economy that cuts back on job security and welfare. Children and adolescents are grappling with mental health issues, addictive behaviour, and substance abuse.

The numerous challenges posed by the COVID-19 lockdowns have both reversed and even exacerbated many of the gains made over the year. In the face of the digital divide, the economic crisis, during COVID-19 we have seen, children have dropped out of school, many have been forced into labour; there has been increase in domestic violence, child abuse, and child marriage, all of these are the areas in where we had started to make some gains.

The lack of access to online education during COVID-19 had a deep impact. Children who were attending schools dropped out and many never got enrolled at all.[12] The ASER 2020[13] report revealed[14] that 5.3 per cent of rural children aged 6-10 years have not enrolled in school this year, compared to 1.8 per cent in 2018. A rapid pilot survey by the National Coalition on the Education Emergency

(NCEE)[15] of poor parents in Karnataka, Telangana and Tamil Nadu to document the experiences during the initial months of schools re-opening, after 18 months of uninterrupted school closures. It found that between 70 and 80 per cent of households felt that their children's ability to read and write had declined or stayed the same (p.7).

There is a change in the ecosystem for those working for social change and child rights too. For decades, human rights activists, small and big non-governmental organisations (NGOs), community-based organisations (CBOs) reached where government could not, monitored and held governments at different levels, empowered communities to speak or spoke on their behalf. It was an important role that they played. Some of these were groups based on strong ideological positions, while others function more in the charity or welfare mode. But this is fast changing.

In the light of this scenario, when the Union Budget 2023-24 was announced, we were not just concerned, but shocked. HAQ: Centre for Child Rights'[16] analysis shows that the Union Budget allocation for children was the lowest in the last 12 years, down from an average 5 per cent to 2.30 per cent, despite the impact of COVID-19. The budget allocations for key ministries too have reduced—Ministry of Women and Child Development, the nodal ministry for children, dropped by 2.54 per cent, Ministry of Labour and Employment that deals with child labour by 33 per cent, and Ministry of Minority Affairs reduced by 37.81 per cent.

Adding to this, we find that in the age of specialisations and technical expertise, the child is getting lost in 'competing' interests. Funding support to carry forward the work is becoming a challenge. Government is increasingly suspicious of 'rights based' groups and even coming down on them. With the entry of corporations into the social sector through its Corporate Social Responsibility Funding, rights-based work has taken a beating. In this environment of mistrust created around NGOs, and the lack of resources to support their work, especially for those that work with a human rights lens, they are struggling to survive.

We are lucky in this country that we have demographic dividend, but what are we doing to nurture and cherish it and build on it. It's said—children are our future. Indeed, they are the adults of tomorrow. But more importantly, they are the citizens today and how we treat them today will determine the future of India.

Children and young people are a part of the ecosystem that we as adults provide them. Are we nurturing, supporting, and guiding our future generations? Are we, providing a value framework that allows them to grow and develop into responsible citizens? Unfortunately, we find that children are violent, aggressive, intolerant, and discriminatory—all because of what they see around them.

It is important to recognise children's citizenship as Indians of today. We must guarantee them rights that the Constitution of India promises to them today and now. It's only when we build on their 'now', they'd be able to be adults of tomorrow. Unfortunately, the ecosystem that we are providing to them is not the kind of nurturing one that they need to grow and develop.

Children are not homogeneous. They are divided by caste, religion, ethnicity, region, gender, ability & disability etc. All this impacts them in different ways. Therefore, one brush stroke for all will not work. That is why what we see our children today are confused, are depressed, they have high levels of addictions, substance abuse; we find them behaving in a manner which are discriminatory and often violent. What are the role models we are providing for them and therefore, I ask myself often, can this change? And I believe that this is possible. Because I would not be the activist that I am if I would not believe in change; I am an eternal optimist, and I believe that the hope lies in our young citizens of today.

Mahatma Gandhi had said:

> The greatest lessons of life, if we would but stoop and humble

> ourselves, we would learn not from grown-up learned men, but from the so-called ignorant children (London, 28 October 1931).

The dreams and aspirations of our children and young people are changing. We need to listen to them providing them with platforms that encourage them to speak freely without fear, and express dissent. But that can happen only when we as adults value constructive criticism. We need an environment that will breed an independent thinking, fearless generation to take forward the democracy we wish to be.

Divided as they are by gender, caste, religion, ethnicity, region or (dis)ability, it is critical that no child is excluded from accessing services. This needs a sound data collection and monitoring mechanism that tracks those who are left out. The government must remember that it has committed to 'Leave No One Behind' (LNOB), a basic principle of the Sustainable Development Goals (SDG). This means guaranteeing inclusion and non-discrimination. More stringent laws may appease public demand for retribution, but cannot be the solution to complex social problems. That lies in investment in social change behaviour, in better access to justice and basic services.

India has made a beginning. As mentioned before, for the first time in 11th Five Year Plan had a separate section on children. This was a real revelation for the country because for the first-time children were recognised as people who needed to be given a place in the planning process. But including them in a chapter or making a scheme or policy is not enough. It is important that children's issues become a part of the developmental indicators and planning. Whether we are creating smart cities or designing mining policies or planning infrastructure projects—everything impacts children. Even forest policies and agriculture policies, which apparently seem disconnected form children's issues, actually impact them. It is well known that the nutrition of children living in the forest fell when people's access to forest were denied. And yet forests are seen as only to be an environmental issue, and not a children's issue. Similarly, agriculture polices too impact children—what is grown impacts what children eat, we have seen how the planting of BT cotton has led to increase in child labour and of course its impact with respect to farmer suicides impact children immediately.

In the same vein, how roads are built, we need to see if children can walk on them. When developmental projects are created, will children be participating in them, will they get gained from them. These are the questions we need to ask us. Therefore, all socio-economic assessments must include the impact on children.

Most important of all, we must be able to help children and young people to grow up as citizens that the framers of our Constitution would have wished, for them to be tolerant, non-discriminatory, responsible, and accountable.

The aspiration of our children and young people are changing, they have different dreams from us. We need to be able to listen to them and provide them with platforms in which they can speak freely and without fear. Can we teach them to differ, to be able to dissent and not feel that it is bad of wrong to be able to be different, this is only possible if we as adults value dissent? If they grow up in a world or a country where adults live in fear, and dissent is punished, then we will not have independent thinking, fearless young people who will take forward the democracy, we so treasure.

Laws are important. But laws alone cannot create social change. Unfortunately, the solution to all crimes against children has been to enact more and more penal law. In fact, every incident of crime brings forth a shrill cry from the society asking for more and more stringent laws. The easiest thing for a country or the state to create another law. But the solution does not lie in creating more laws, as that it's not what leads to social change. Solution to all crimes against children cannot be retribution. We are already witnessing impact of these 'populist' laws on the lives of children. What was anticipated as 'problems' with the amendments by experts and practitioners, leading to protest and controversy, is already a reality. What is lost in all of this is justice and protection of children—the very purpose of these laws. What is needed is the timely delivery of justice, rightful conviction and restoring the sense of justice to the victim. For that we need a change of attitude both towards the child victims, and perhaps towards the children who offend.

Children are not born as offenders or criminals. They are imbibing what we are teaching them or what we are showing them since they are part of the ecosystem that I referred to earlier. They often emulate the adults.

Let us invest resources, time and most importantly, our faith in children and young people so they can help us to lead the change.

Today's children are adults of tomorrow. And they will build and live in an India that we show them is possible. If we engage with them, nurture them and help them uphold the Constitutional values, we will have India, which my parents had fought as freedom fighters, and many like them dreamt for.

NOTES

1 This article is an expanded version of the talk I had given as part of ANHAD's 'Reimagining India' series of lectures.

2 Ganguly, Santi Pada, *Significance in the Insignificant: My Childhood Memoirs*, New York: Mimeo, pp.31-32

3 *Deccan Herald*, 'India ranks 15th in policies, practices against child sexual violence: Report', 25 September 2022

4 *The Indian Express*, 'India has seen steady decline in child marriages', 3 November 2022

5 Shukla, Subir, *Education as a Right*, 2019, p.107, https://www.haqcrc.org/publication/indias-children-continue-to-challenge-our-conscience/

6 https://hlrn.org.in/documents/Forced_Evictions_2021.pdf

7 *The Print*, '"Reverse dowry", rape & "good houses of bad husbands"—the hidden stories of Gujarat's child brides', 14 June 2023

8 *The Logical Indian*, 'World Day Against Trafficking: 8000 Children Trafficked

in Last 3 Years in India, What is the Current Situation?', 30 July 2022

9 https://www.globalhungerindex.org/pdf/en/2022/India.pdf

10 https://www.globalhungerindex.org/pdf/en/2022/India.pdf

11 https://www.undp.org/sites/g/files/zskgke326/files/2022-10/2022mpi reportenpdf.pdf

12 *India Today*, 'How COVID-19 has forced the dropout rate to shoot up in India and what we can do', 21 November 2021

13 Annual Status of Education Report (Rural) 2020, Wave 1, Provisional, 28 October 2020

14 *The Hindu*, 'Nearly 20% of rural school children had no textbooks due to COVID-19 impact, finds ASER survey', 28 October 2020

15 https://educationemergency.net/2022/03/cries-of-anguish/

16 https://www.haqcrc.org/wp-content/uploads/2023/02/BfC-Analysis_2023-24.pdf

Some Feminist Dreams for the Future

Nivedita Menon

As we all know, this is an unprecedented time for our country. There is complete subversion of the Constitution, the selling of India's public assets to private capital, the privatising of higher education, innumerable physical attacks against Dalits and religious minorities, especially Muslims, policing of women, and the use of labels like 'love jihad' to basically control women's sexuality and mobility—to name just some of the kinds of violence we face today. Even the pandemic and the lockdown, as we know, were weaponised in order to push through the dual agenda of this regime of establishing a violent, authoritarian Hindu Rashtra and promoting crony capitalism. But, that is not the point of this discussion today. Today, I would like us to dream of beautiful things, of another world, of other worlds, of something hopeful for the future.

What can we work towards? What kinds of resources do we already have? What can we build? What are our dreams and visions for our children? I hope to arrive at some of these ideas from the perspective of a queer leftist feminist whose understanding is deeply informed by Ambedkarite thinking and politics. There are of course, many, many things we can talk about but for the purpose of this brief discussion, I will pick up three issues and talk about how we could be reimagining them, not only from the point of view of what the state and the government can do, but also from the point of view of our own self transformations. What are the ways in which we, as a movement and as individuals, can transform the society?

The first point I want to take up is how feminists look at the sexual division of labour and how it globally undergirds not only patriarchy but also class and caste inequalities. Now, what do we mean by the sexual division of labour? It is the division of work, a conceptual division of work into the 'private' and the 'public'. It is the conceptual understanding that the work of production and the work of reproduction should be sexually divided. The work of reproduction involves not just pregnancy and giving birth to new labour power or labouring bodies; it also includes the reproduction of labour power by which strength of the labour is replenished. Reproduction is assumed to be in the 'private' domain and production is to be in the 'public' domain.

Now, of course, we all know that most women actually function in both domains and what we are thinking of as the private domain is actually very public because this unwaged labour is what lies at the basis of profits for employers as they are not paying for a large part of what the worker needs. So sexual division of labour ensures that women perform this labour. Either they do it for free in their own homes or they perform this work for a pittance in other people's homes as well as in their own homes.

Those who perform domestic work as wage labourers are not only poor, but are often from the non *Savarna* castes. They could be Dalits or OBCs, but even if they are not, there is a definite caste division in the performance of this labour. The implicit caste dimensions and the assumptions of untouchability that cling to domestic labour are evident in the way they are called 'servants' and treated as such in middle class homes. They don't sit on chairs but on the floor; don't eat from the same vessels as the family they work for, and are often not even permitted to use lifts and toilets in the home. So there is an implicit caste construction in the way domestic wage labour is positioned in the frameworks of pollution and purity, touchability and untouchability. This is what sexual division of labour produces, in a sense. So, what is our alternative vision? What is the way in which we can rethink this?

To begin with, we need to recognise that sexual division of labour is as much of a compulsorily and violently enforced institution as caste is, and not optional or voluntarily chosen. Women who refuse to perform this labour are controlled very strictly by families and society, and are often physically coerced into adhering to the norms. This compulsory institution ensures that all women are affected in their public roles to some extent. If they are higher up in the class ladder, they are affected by it to a lesser extent than women who belong to the lower rungs of class. So, how to address this situation?

Firstly, we need to recognise it as a violent and compulsory institution for one can only dismantle something once it is recognised it for what it is.

Once this happens, we can work towards dismantling it, to begging with, in our own lives. One way of doing it is by committing to paying a fair living wage to those who perform this labour at our homes so that they don't have to do this back breaking work in four separate houses just to keep them away from starving. If there is one thing that the Indian middle class has understood during the lockdown, then it is the excruciating nature of household work which the domestic workers perform for them. We have to commit to paying a living wage to those who do this work so that they can actually make a dignified life for themselves. We need to, in a kind of a broader way, work towards social and state, and employers' responsibility for domestic labour and child care facilities at all workplaces. In other words, the responsibility for child care should be treated as a social and public responsibility. State resources should be poured into child care facilities at all work sites, not just government worksites.

We often use the term 'human resources' for people, although I wouldn't like to use that term. However, if these 'resources' are to be used by the state, then the state and society also have a responsibility for ensuring that these facilities are available at all workplaces. Such a compulsion will generate a kind of ripple effect of employment. There will be women (and perhaps men depending on the comfort level of parents) employed at child care facilities. The children of those women who are running the child care facilities or doing the work in the child care facilities, should also have a place in those facilities. This should be something like a common minimum programme for all political interests across the board. This means we would be talking about a world in which domestic labour is taken as something that is foundational to the building of society.

The second issue that I will address is that of sexual violence and sexual harassment and how do we engage with these in a world which we would like to look different from the one we currently live in. So here we would press for the need for state-run public transport which should be ideally free, but at least cheap. It should be publicly funded and cover all parts of a city or town and be available for 24 hours so that it is possible for more people to be on the roads at all times. One of the things that feminists have been arguing for a long time is that sexual harassment in public places is reduced when more women are on the roads or in public spaces at all times. Increased accessibility of public transport will obviously have some repercussions for environmental pollution, but overall it is a good move in more than one direction, and by reducing private transport usage has implications for pollution as well.

And now our responsibility would be to address sexual harassment and violence in every space that we are in. Each of us is responsible for making sure that the environment is not one of sexual harassment or violence, in our homes, in streets, in institutions where we work. This can be done by introducing procedures and ways of dealing with such acts as and when these happen before us. The law is not always the answer. The existing law needs to be transformed. The 2013 law has several problems, which we cannot go into now. The Justice Verma Committee recommendations were in fact much, much more reflective of the kind of inputs that the different social movements, particularly the feminist groups, contributed. A 'one-size-fits-all' kind of law cannot take care of sexual harassment in spaces and institutions as varied as a university, a factory, an office and so on. The only way in which we can deal with sexual violence is by making sure that there are multiple regulations in multiple institutions to suit specific work conditions. We also need to work towards a system that would support the complainant without impunity and ensure accountability. What we don't need is strong punishments. We don't need death sentences. We don't need longer imprisonment spells. It has been well established that stricter punishments do not lead to reduction of crime. It does not act as a deterrent. What we need is certainty and quickness of punishment if someone is found guilty. It does not matter whether the case is at the level of an internal sexual harassment committee or at the level of courts, it cannot drag on for 7 years, 8 years, 15 years. Bhanwari Devi[1] still hasn't got justice decades down the line. So we need to ensure a legal system in which there is immediate dealing with the situation, certainty of punishment and timely execution of the same.

We do need to think differently about sexual violence in the context of let's say rape of Dalit women or Muslim women in situations of communal violence, and here of course, the state has to intervene and take prompt action against the perpetrators. The local police, who are often found to be closely involved with and act in the interests of the perpetrators in such cases, as we saw in Hathras,[2] should be trained to do otherwise. We do have to remember that rapes of Dalit women are one more way of reinforcing the caste order and the violence of caste. So it's not only rape, it's not only about women, it is about re-establishing caste violence too. This is part of the strategy, and the tactic of controlling and maintaining caste hierarchy. So we have to, at our level, work both towards institutional changes as well as changes on the ground, such that we create a society in which sexual violence is made recognisable, prevented as far as possible, and punished promptly when it does take place.

Women should not have to offer reasons for being in public. Women should not have to offer reasons for just loitering, in a park, in the streets, in Connaught Place (Delhi), or just walking into any public area and just hanging out.

Even women who bear class privilege are not able to come out of policing. Working class women in working class localities are very strictly policed as much as upper-class women are. While some upper-class women manage to escape these constraints, young women growing up in poor localities are strictly policed and controlled. So, we need to think about public spaces—how to make them joyous, heterogeneous and accessible not only in terms of gender, but also in terms the disabled and the marginalised. It is an alternative dream, a vision where we want to counter and contest and transform societies which are driven by sexual violence.

In this new world, we aspire to create systems in which those who face sexual violence are taken seriously and are supported. For example, sexual violence directed at a transwoman must be taken as seriously as sexual violence against any other gender. So as far as sexual violence is concerned, we are thinking in terms of building joyous public spaces. People who are usually on the margins or have disability can freely enter there. That's one kind of thing; the other kind of thing is working towards transforming both the law as well as institutional procedures so that there is certainty of punishment, and the surety of a short yet quick process by which the case is examined. Lastly, we are thinking about a way in which conversations on sexual violence and harassment shift in a way that what is rendered normal—objectification of human bodies—becomes unacceptable.

The third issue, and this is the final issue that I will be talking about, has to do with sexuality and the family. So gender justice in the household and what does it mean to live in a world in which we value and support all kinds of intimate relationships, not just the heterosexual nuclear marriage system, but all forms of ways in which human beings want to live in intimacy with one another, support one another—all of these need to be valued, supported, have legal recognition wherever necessary. All forms of family, all kinds of gender identities, all kinds of sexual orientation, sexual desires, all of these. And in order to question the institution of compulsory heterosexual marriage framework and to recognise and accept multiple ways in which people can live in intimacy and solidarity and in love with one another in as many numbers as they need. It could be people living alone, it could be people living in communities, it could be people living in couples, but the point is, human beings have multiple ways of entering into intimacy. And the overarching and very violent institution of compulsory marriage is something we definitely need to challenge. Now, marriage can always be reconstituted and there are people who will continue to want to enter into marriage; and in that case if there is such a thing as a legal institution of marriage then that has to be based on a mutual contract between adults, not between families, as is the case now.

The word contract is often used to make something sound unemotional and devoid of value but no, this is simply used to indicate that marriage is a legal relationship, which has property implications, which has income implications, implications for who will have custody of the children, because of course I think we will have to recognise that more and more, it will not be one marriage in a lifetime. Relationships may end and they may change. We have to be prepared for that. So, in that case, the contract will recognise and should recognise what the economic share of each partner is, recognise that reproductive labour has value, it should have clarity on how the marriage contract can be ended, what are the equitable ways in which the common property can be shared, how are children to be treated. There is another interesting implication arising from thinking about what an equitable marriage contract could look like, and that is for the Uniform Civil Code debate. Because when uniformity is stressed as something that is good for everybody, we need to recognise that uniformity is not in fact justice. Uniformity does not mean Equality. Uniformity only means that everybody has to be the same. As what? Same as who? What will be the norm on the basis of which everybody has to be the same? If that question is asked, you will find that those norms are the dominant norms, the powerful community norms, the most patriarchal, the most casteist, those are the norms that will be rendered uniform across the board. So we really need to accept that as feminists, a lot of feminists have been arguing, for example in Africa, that legal pluralism is not itself a bad thing.

There are heterogeneous kinds of gender injustice, and therefore, there should be multiple ways of engaging with these legally.

We don't need uniformity, we need gender justice, we need legal and social codes that ensure not just gender justice but also challenge the caste and class inequality that undergirds the present system.

So, in short, to conclude, we will build a world in which we work, from our personal and private spaces outwards; that is, from the personal and private spaces in which we are located; we move outwards, we refuse to participate in the assembling of the current social order; we just keep dismantling it one layer, one thread at a time, and gradually the very ground shifts...

Aur ek din pata bhi nahi chala ke kaise badlaav aaya[3]

NOTES

1 Bhanwari Devi was gang-raped in 1992 by upper-caste men in whose family she had prevented a child marriage, in her capacity as an employee of a government programme. The district and sessions court in Jaipur dismissed the case and acquitted all the five accused in 1995, on the grounds that it was impossible that upper-caste men would even touch a Dalit woman, let alone rape her. The case was then appealed in the Rajasthan High Court where it has languished without progress since then. However, Bhanwari Devi has become an icon of the feminist movement and her experience inspired the feminist intervention that resulted in the Vishaka guidelines by the Supreme Court on sexual harassment at the workplace.

2 In 2020, a Dalit woman in the Hathras village of Uttar Pradesh (UP) was allegedly gang-raped by four upper-caste men. She eventually succumbed to her injuries. The incident created a lot of media stir since the victim's body was said to have been forcibly cremated by the police without the consent of her family, and there was no arrest made in the initial 10 days. However, the SC/ST Court acquitted three of the four accused. The fourth man has been found guilty of culpable homicide not amounting to murder, but not rape.

3 And suddenly one day, we didn't even know it, but change had happened!

Education

Reinventing the University of Teaching and Research

Dhruv Raina

There has been a lot of discussion recently on the New Education Policy. The discussion began shortly after an early draft of it was circulated. Though I am not going to talk about the document itself, but would like to talk about the future, or the likely futures of higher education in particular, with reference to some of the suggestions and policy claims made in this document. The starting point would be the strongest claim which is often made, that one of its goals is the decolonisation of education itself, and of higher education in particular. I would start out by saying that it depends on what one means by decolonisation, and there are at least three different aspects to decolonisation.

The first, of course, relates to the democratisation of higher education, the second relates to issues of connectivity and the third has to do with plurality and diversity. It is not possible to look at the future of higher education without keeping these three concerns in mind. If we look at the long history of the university in India, we would see that it has consistently contributed to the task of nation building. Towards the last decades of the 20th century, the Indian universities facilitated mobility of students and professionals who migrated to other places to seek employment there. So, the universities were also preparing an international cadre of highly trained professionals. Today, it makes sense to touch upon this less discussed task of the university, because, we have recognised in the light of the pandemic as well as the major climatic changes which have been taking place, that we also have to think about planetary futures, and that when we plan for our education, we are not just planning for the task of nation building, but we are planning for the task of living in a deeply, highly connected world.

Are we thinking along these lines when we discuss higher education and the decolonisation of higher education? Are we thinking about these connectivities? Are we thinking about planetary futures? These are some of the issues I think we need to talk about in reimagining the future of the university. The issue of democracy, the issue of connectivity, and the issue of plurality and diversity. And of course, very often, this plurality and diversity in some quarters, is understood to mean divisiveness, rather than contributing both to the enrichment of culture, and of perspectives, and different points of view. One can make an argument from this, from the philosophies of science, but that is not something I would go into, on this occasion. That's something to be discussed at another moment. So, how does one think that higher education contributes to decolonisation? This is certaily not a new agenda on the menu of higher education. It goes back to the last decades of the 19th century, and one definition of decolonisation is the dis-identification with colonial practices and constructions.

The modern university system that was first established in India in 1857, started off as an examining body. And from the 1870s onwards, beginning with the Indian Association for the Cultivation of Sciences (Kolkata), there was a long struggle which went on amongst those who were getting educated to finally establish a university of teaching and learning. The demand for a university that emphasised on teaching and research was the first moment of decolonisation. And today we don't seem to realise that over a century, what we have developed in India is a very complex ecology, highly differentiated with the multiplicity of functions, at different levels, because as a society becomes more complex, as production functions differentiate, the system of knowledge production also differentiates to a great degree. Today we'd like to refer to ourselves as a knowledge society. If we are indeed a knowledge society, then, are we going to basically separate the teaching functions from research functions? Or are we going to say that we wish to further develop and elaborate upon this structure we have taken a long time to develop, rather than say, we should have colleges for teaching, and we should have separate research institutes? Are we aware of all that is at stake in discussing what was referred to as the unity of teaching and research. Contemporary thinking on the subject has also been, in a way, driven by certain assumptions about the neoliberal argument for separating the teaching function from the research function of a university. Universities have become very big these days but only a small percentage of students who go through the university basically end up in research positions as most of them go on to perform other functions within society. The second assumption is that in the university of teaching and research, no matter what you do, you're trained to be a researcher and that doesn't necessarily square with the requirements of society.

This by itself cannot become the logic for separating teaching and research in a university. There are reasons enough, both at the global and national levels, to think that the university of teaching and research is under threat and although the government has constantly said that funding for research will not come down, we have seen that happening in the last few years. India used to be a kind of model for third world countries in the late 1990s. Researchers from other parts of the third world often remarked that the way India allocates funds in research is commendable for as close to one per cent of our GDP got invested solely for research. Though it was nowhere near the four per cent of the GDP of the American economy, or the Korean economy, but, it was still significant for a third world country like India to invest in building scientific and research establishments, on which the skills of the society would develop.

There's much criticism of the policies of the 1950s and the commitment to higher education and in the development of a scientific and technological system. The system may have been sub-optimal but it did pay dividends, even if it were a bit late. In that sense, the concern is not that those policies did not pay but that the impact was delayed impact. In fact, whatever was invested in higher education in the 1950s and 1960s, started paying off in the 1980s and the 1990s. If India has now joined the information economy in such a significant way, it's also a result of those policies. Consequently, we have to learn to look at the research system as a highly differentiated system full of connections. But this way of looking at the system does not dismiss the vocationalisation of education, which is one of the instruments of the new education policy. What needs to be recognised is that you cannot promote the vocationalisation of education, at the cost of either dismantling or under emphasising the importance of the scientific and technological research system, because all the components of the system are deeply connected. If you make a small change in one, you can end up destroying or undermining another component of this system. And, so, one has to look at the kinds of linkages which already exist and extend from the realm of higher secondary education, to undergraduate education, postgraduate education, and then, research.

So, that's one part of the argument. The second part of the argument has to do with the fact that, even if we look at the system of higher education and research, there are institutions of national importance where advanced research is indeed done and, where researchers are connected with the frontiers of science in different parts of the world. Then there are the Central Universities, and the under-funded State Universities, and the difference in levels of research among these is indeed quite substantial. It could be argued that the National Education Policy should focus on building research capacities at State Universities, so that they can become responsive to state level needs and can gradually bridge the gap between these three tiers—the under-funded, understaffed State level universities, the less funded central universities, and the well-funded universities of research and teaching.

This is not an either-or proposition, because the well-funded universities and institutes of research have very often felt that the quality of students sometimes coming in from the central universities or the state universities into the institutions of national importance has been declining. But it has been declining why? Some measures have been put in place to rectify some of these defects, but a lot more has to be done. Now one can take two attitudes. To build new institutions, or on the other hand to reform slowly and improvise and fund already existing structures. How is this to be done? It's not a question of how you look at research institutions, or how you look at higher education. Institutions of higher education take a long period of nursing; they have long gestation periods. To build a good tradition of research and teaching takes a long time. You can't build them overnight. So, there is a need to look back and reflect upon which were our successes and what can we learn from those successes? And what were our failures and what can we learn from them? And then try to reinvigorate our state-level institutions and those central universities which have gone into decline.

Social justice is not possible without cognitive justice. The reverse is also true: cognitive justice is not possible without social justice. What has this to do with higher education? The point acquires salience, because all those who are now talking about the privatisation of higher education in India basically acquired their own education at public institutions, and now there is this move to abandon these public institutions and replace them with, or substitute them with private institutions, which may well be beyond the resources of the majority of the population. Can we achieve social justice like this? In order to achieve social justice, we have to deliver on cognitive justice. And that role was performed to an extent in our public institutions, but the new education policy seems to achieve cognitive justice, perhaps at the cost of social justice. So, we have to basically re-look at the strategies of privatisation, or the lack of support for public institutions. Can we undermine the systems of public institutions? We all know that our parents, who emphasised the importance of higher education for us, studied in public institutions. What is the status of government schools today? The question needs to be posed to all who acquired education in public funded institutions—are we going to undermine these public funded institutions and replace them with private institutions?

This issue was flagged because we cannot create a just knowledge society, unless higher education is widespread in a way that it contributes towards the enrichment of the system of higher education. So, in discussing the decolonisation of higher education, it cannot only mean the indigenisation of higher education, because the system of higher education today, is a globally connected one. When you look at some of the debates on decolonisation in Africa, it is also seen as an opening out into the world. It is about connectivities. Since we have to consider planetary futures and simultaneously manage the task of nation building by producing a cadre of highly trained professionals who can ensure a sustainable future, we have to think then in terms of a cosmopolitics of education. And of course, the National Education Policy, while talking of diversity, has probably not paid enough attention to these aspects of higher education.

In conclusion it is important to stress the concern about the differentiation of the system of higher education in a way that it reflects an attempt to engage with the diversity of Indian cultures, and of course, also to engage with the place of India in a globalised world. We are thinking of a nation which is culturally diverse, but we are also thinking of a world which is culturally diverse, so, we also have to think about how do we sustain such a world which is marred by conflict? Education must provide us the means of thinking through these conflicts. The National Education Policy should give us some indication, as to how are we going to deal with a planetary future and how do we negotiate the task between building such a diverse nation on the one hand, and simultaneously contributing towards producing a cadre of trained professionals who can work with people across different national contexts, in building a sustainable future.

A Vision for Indian Science

Gautam Menon

Whenever we talk of reimagining Indian science, an interesting question we can ask is what do we think of Indian science in the future? What sort of shape would we want it to take? Do we imagine it to be better integrated with the science that is done worldwide or will we have the opportunity to reimagine it and to change it altogether? What parts of it could we change? Indian science looks very much like the practice of science in other countries. We have a large university system. We have research institutes and robust space and nuclear programmes. We have an extensive agricultural research programme. But, if we look into the depth of all these, carefully inside, cracks begin to appear. Our students who graduate in large numbers, are mostly not employable at the level that we would like them to be. Not all of them are creative, independent, individual members of the community as we would like them to be after having achieved a certain level of education. That's where it's important to think about how we could change the structure of science education. I want to discuss the state of science education in India in the light of COVID-19 epidemic. There's no doubt that India, as well as many other countries of the world, have been through an experience that is unparalleled. This makes it a good time to think about what is it that we can do, given what we have learned so far, and how we should reimagine what we have so that we can construct a better future for us and for everyone else in this country.

So, as I said, COVID-19 has given us an opportunity to think about many of these questions more carefully. And it's important to realise the crucial role that science has played in our understanding of COVID-19 and our ability to deal with it. We have done things that we never thought would be possible. We have developed vaccines within the span of a year when the normal timescale for developing a vaccine is 20 years or so. We have been able to identify the causative agent of COVID-19, the SARS CoV 2 virus, within the span of about 5-6 days and were able to figure out the sequence of the DNA of the RNA molecule that was inside it and turn that into a device that we could use to swiftly diagnose cases of COVID-19 when they appear in the community. These are things that we could not have anticipated earlier. In order to achieve this, one required input from pretty much every branch of science to come together and also required large amounts of government support.

In the background of the Pandemic, here are ten points that describe how I think we might reconfigure Indian science for the future. There may be some disagreement on what these points are, and someone else might come up with a different set of points, but I nevertheless hope that there will be some level of overlap in what I think of and what you might think of as a scientist or as a member of the lay public. My points are centred around what we would like a society to be in future, in order to create a more fair, equitable society where the rights of everyone is taken into account.

So, my first point is understanding the role of science is crucial to becoming a better citizen. By better citizen, I don't mean someone who is just mechanically obeying the laws of the country, as they might be, but someone who thinks about why those laws are and how these help to protect the rights of everyone in this country. To do that, one must introduce scientific methods and scientific ways of thinking in the way they deal with the world. When I say scientific methods of thinking, what I really mean is understanding the role of evidence. How does one accumulate evidence, make sense of it and act upon it? Evidence-based medicine, evidence-based science, evidence-based policy is central to understanding these questions of how one makes a better citizen in a democracy. There is a common superstition that looking at an eclipse harms pregnant women, what evidence is there for that? What happens in regions of the world which may see an eclipse versus those which don't see an eclipse? Is there a difference between them? How would we test it? These are questions where science can actually contribute a methodological understanding of what should be believed and what part of knowledge should be discarded on the basis of lack of evidence.

The second important point that I think is particularly crucial now in the background of the COVID-19 epidemic is that we must break the barriers and boundaries between the different sciences. The identification and management of COVID-19 rests on this multi-pronged approach to science that experts took—techniques in physics, for example, electron microscopy that could tell you about the structure of the Coronavirus and identify this virus as a particular type of Coronavirus, methods in vaccinology, methods in clinical medicine—all these together enabled the treatment of COVID-19. The PCR test was originally devised in a completely different context but is now commonly used in order to find out if one suffers from COVID-19 or not. The breakthroughs across the domains of sciences are important but it's also important to understand the relationship of the sciences to the social sciences. That's another barrier that one must break. The sciences cannot exist on their own. Also, it is important to communicate the results of science and its importance, the philosophical thinking around science to the lay public at large. So, in order to become a better citizen, it's not sufficient to think only about science. One must think about the social impacts of science and the social consequences of it.

My third point has to do with the importance of local community-based concerns and needs centred around ecology, sustainability, and conservation. There are parts of India that are among the most biodiverse in the world. Even though they're being eaten at by various types of commercial interests it would tend to shrink them. Now, more than ever before, it is important to be cognisant of our ecology, of the rich diversity of life that surrounds us. Not just for reasons that we might choose to plunder them at some point, but because they may supply to us vital sources of new drugs, of new medicines, of new knowledge, of new potential inspirations for constructing things, man-made objects that derive their inspiration from biological and living systems. In order to do that, one must start with the community and the problem it faces in terms of pollution, disasters, etc, and then move outward to a larger extent to see how these problems affect the district, the state, the nation as a whole. So, rooting these in the local community is an important part of what science can do.

My fourth point is an expansion of the third point—the concern for local communities and ecology. The problems that the world faces with global warming, overfishing, etc, are not problems of any single locality only. They're not problems of America versus India versus Russia versus Japan. These are wicked problems because they involve the interaction of different factors and there are combined interests as well. It's impossible to think of climate change as a responsibility just of one country. No country can keep its pollution to itself. Changes in our climate can originate in parts of North America but then very rapidly spread to other parts of the world. It's our responsibility as a nation to be aware of our own part in creating these large global changes to our climate, to our environment and understand our own role in contributing to that as well as our own role as being part of a global scheme that sets these matters in motion.

My fifth point has to do with the importance of reimagining our approach to health and disease. The pandemic, more than anything else, has taught us the importance of a good public health system. India is home to the largest number of stunted children in the world. We are home to lots of neglected tropical diseases which are not the interest of, for example, Western population because they don't experience these. If India does not solve these problems for itself no one will solve these for us. Let me also describe the importance of involving communities in this effort. How do we become sensitive to a new disease that appears somewhere? At what level can community participation help us identify what might be happening. To what extent can communities partner with a good public health system to provide early warnings of what might be happening in the future? To what extent can communities be involved in science that leads to those outcomes and the science that leads to understanding public health and the determinants of public health a little better because these should be community concerns. Involving local communities in constructing public health systems, ensuring that good public health is available to any citizen of India, wherever they happen to be are important aspects in determining the nature of science and the nature of medicine as applied to our population and what we should reimagine the future.

My sixth point has to do with the nature of appropriate science and innovation. Let me give you an example. The 'Foldscope' is a remarkable invention. It was made by an Indian scientist based in the US. And it is a little microscope that you can construct essentially out of very simple components put together cheaply. This is a microscope that enables you to do as much as a regular microscope at a lesser expense made of metal which you might buy in a shop, and is of course, out of the reach of many of the students in our population. How do we think about making science easy in this country that is still developing? How do we go away from looking at big science as being the only science worthwhile of doing? And how do we look at extending the freedom to look scientifically at problems of every citizen in the country? I think the way lies in discovering that appropriate science is not always big science, but right science, the kind that involves things that anyone can do.

My seventh point relates to the importance of Mathematics. This is often ignored in discussions of science. But there's no doubt that an understanding of Mathematics and a love for the same is the foundation of pretty much any science that you can think of. It lies at the foundation of the GPS system that one can use to figure out directions. It is at the base of predictions the kind of which we saw during the COVID-19 times—understanding the nature of how the virus might change, how different variants might appear and which might be more serious and which might be milder, so on and so forth. Mathematics is the bedrock of all of these. Removing the fear of Mathematics in young children, in older students, and even with adults is an important thing to do for our country.

My eighth point is bridging the gap between basic and applied science. When we think of science, we often think of basic science as the important science. But basic science is of no use unless it has something to be applied to. And applied science can only function on the profound basis of good basic science. So, while we should continue to support basic science in this country, it is important for us to also connect to applied science. Applied science, that can be taken to the people, can also be used in ways that are appropriate to our country and to our communities.

My ninth point may seem a little unusual, and that has to do with the relationship between science and religion. In a country where more than 90% of people believe in some form of organised religion, it has traditionally been the job of science to stay away from questions that have to do with religion. But it's important to understand the role of private belief. And scientists, more than anyone else, should also be cognisant of this boundary and able to present this in a way that establishes what science is all about and how it should not interfere with private belief. This is important because science and private belief should not be understood as a conflict, but the difference between what can be established using a knowledge base and what really is a private observance.

My last point is probably my most important point, and that has to do with education and reimagining education and the importance of teachers. None of what I have said is even remotely possible if we did not have teachers who supported the practice of science. It's important to train, empower and support good teachers. It's important to teach teachers about the frontiers of science and where science is actually going. We should pay teachers better because they're fundamental to creating new generation of people. Teachers can create students who can think for themselves, who are independent, and have the potential to become citizens of the type that we would like to encourage—thinking and conscious citizens who are aware of their place in the democracy. Again, this may not look like science, but it's crucial to create the sort of people that we want in the next generation.

We have traditionally, as a society, valued credentials over actual learning. What are the children learning? What are young people learning? How do we make sure that they incorporate the principles and the ideas of the science in what they're learning to make them more independent and on their own? I think this is, as I said, the most important in the creation of good teachers and the understanding of the value that they bring to our society.

Health

Towards an Efficient and Equitable Health System

K Srinath Reddy

In a world that is being battered by COVID-19, we are now looking forward to better times. We would need to build our health systems better, broader and fairer because we cannot go back to old systems, which have failed us. Indeed, COVID-19 has given us many lessons.

1. Health systems, which are not efficient and equitable to begin with in the steady state before the pandemic failed to create a swift and strong surge response in the face of public health emergency. Counties and states of India which had better public health systems coped better even though they too were challenged with the magnitude of the pandemic.
2. We also recognised that unless countries have a strong public sector presence in their health systems they cannot really discharge the functions of delivering acceptable and affordable health care to the all sections of the people even during periods without an emergency, but particularly during public health emergency the health system cannot function in terms of efficient and equitable delivery of health services.
3. We recognised that primary health care systems are particularly important in terms of building a stronger health system, which can deliver Universal Health Coverage (UHC) to all of its people in any country.

Building on these lessons, we must look at how India has evolved its health system over decades of its independence where the fault lines lie and how can we improve upon the structure functioning and accountability of our health system.

Firstly, we look at where India's health indicators lie. If we are really looking at our health indicators as a reflection of the efficient and equitable dimensions of our system performance, then we have a great deal of cause for concerns. The reasons are simple even if you compare India with the neighbouring countries, we find in India the infant mortality is around 30 per thousand live births whereas in Sri Lanka it's 6, in Bangladesh it's 25 in China it's 7.4. If you look at life expectancy, a cumulative measure of how health is really looked after by the society of all its citizens, then India's life expectancy is 69.2 years. In Sri Lanka it's 77 years, in Bangladesh it's 72 years, in China it's 76.6, even Nepal has higher life expectancy than India.

So, it is not just economic development alone that matters, because we are better developed than our South-Asian neighbours but the manner in which health system is configured to deliver health services to all its citizens in efficient and equitable manner that matters. And here, we must recognise that we have grossly under-invested in our health system in terms of public financing of health. If you look at the comparative expenditure on health across different countries and look at total health expenditure as well as governments' contributions to that health expenditure, then we see that in India, in all the health care expenditure, government contributes only 30%, whereas in Sri Lanka, it's 56%, in China, it's close to 60%, in Brazil, it's 46%, in Japan, it's 83.6%, in Germany it's 77%, and in Thailand it's 77.8%. Even in the United States of America which is seen as a poster child of private health care, the public financing or government expenditure on health care is 48.3%. But in India, it is 30%. As a result, we have a very high level of out of pocket expenditures. India's out of pocket expenditure in the past three decades has hovered between 60-75%. Now it is considered to be closer to 58%. That means, this is what a person has to spend out of pocket for his/her health care. In Sri Lanka it's 42%, in China it's 32%, in Japan it's 14%, in Thailand it's 11.9% and in the UK it's 9.7%.

So, if we really look at how we are faring in out of pocket

expenditure in comparison to other countries, India ranks in top 10 counties. Whereas, in case of government health expenditure in proportion to total health expenditure, India ranks 176 out of 191 countries. It means, if you look at low out of pocket expenditure and rank countries according to that, India is at 182 out of 191 countries. And this is a great cause for concern because under resourced health system cannot perform efficiently to deliver the health care need of its entire people. So, there will be great deal of health problems which will occur particularly among the poorer and vulnerable sections of the society.

If we look at different states of India again, we find there is a considerable difference in the way the states too have been spending on health. And states which have invested more in health and particularly in the delivery of health services through strong public sector like Kerala, Tamil Nadu and some of the other southern states do generally well whereas the states in central, northern India and the northeast, which are under-invested in health and particularly ignored, the public sector has not done well either before or during the pandemic. If you look at the state expenditures of Uttar Pradesh and Bihar, then it is Rs 800-1,000 per capita per person per year whereas in Goa it's 6,000, in Arunachal Pradesh it's 10,000. So, there are differences across the country but in general, if you take the proportion of health as part of overall budget of the states, then some of the southern states have spent much more than the northern and central Indian states. Particularly, the southern states and Himachal Pradesh have focused on strengthening the public sector services.

The insurance schemes are much talked about but do not contribute much. Private Insurance contributes to about 10% while government insurance contributes to about 26.5% of total coverage at the moment. We recognise that many people who do not have financial protection when challenged with severe health care problem, either get catastrophic impact on their finances and are pushed towards poverty and even they have to spend chronically for ailments like blood pressure, diabetes or other conditions which require lifelong care, then out of pocket expenditure again pushes them into poverty. And we have seen this happening, for example, in the different surveys of the National Sample Survey Organisation conducted between 2004 and 2014. Despite the so called health insurance schemes coming up from the government both at the central and state level, 7% of India's population were at the risk of being pushed into poverty because of health care expenditure alone.

This is one of the major causes of poverty in India. And at the same time, apart from the financing aspect of it, we find there is a great deal of asymmetry in the availability of health care providers in India. Overall there is huge shortage all across India but there are huge asymmetries among the states and between urban and rural areas. For example, if you look at the health work force which consists of doctors, nurses, and midwife and of course allied health professionals, the shortage of doctors is evident. Whereas the global norm is one doctor per thousand, we find one doctor per 1,511 persons in India. Similarly, for nurses, it is 1:670 whereas the global norm is 1:500. Combining doctors, nurses and midwives, the World Health Organization estimates that we need 44.5 of these 3 categories of health care providers per ten thousand populations in order to deliver universal health coverage and meet the sustainable development goals. We have just about half that number—22 per 10 thousand—therefore, we do need many more people at various levels right from community health workers to various allied health professionals in medical technicians to basic doctors to specialist doctors and of course, we need to ensure that public health expertise is greatly developed because we have seen how the lack of public health expertise failed us during the COVID-19 pandemic.

So, we must correct some of the gross distortions that exist, but we must also recognise there is a great number of mal-distribution among states. If you take health care work force then we find while 2/3 of the population is living in rural areas, 2/3 of doctors, nurses and allied health works are actually working in urban area. It's exactly the reverse. Even the Indian system of medicine, 'Ayush', is mostly practised in urban areas and very few centres are spread across rural areas. While we have invested in rural primary health care, urban primary health care does not exist in most of the cities in an organised manner and people have to depend upon either private hospitals or the high end tertiary hospitals of the government. About 60% or more of our medical colleges are situated in the four south Indian states and western India whereas in central India, northern India and northeast India, medical colleges are very few in number and do not train adequate number of undergraduate and post graduate doctors. So, we need to correct several of these distortions as we go along.

Let me now come to why this has happened. India started off fairly well with a strong commitment to universal health coverage or care right from the period of Independence. It had strong emphasis on the public sector and we found that whether it was primary care centre or government hospital in the city, care was provided mostly free by the public sector, however, under-resourcing, under-financing of the public sector with also reduced number of people in terms of health work force, poor governance, all of these saw public sector dwindled in terms of its presence and decline in terms of its performance; with economic liberalisation, we saw private sector coming up in a big way starting in 1980s but really roaring into large dominant presence from 1990 onwards. Now, much of the care is provided by the private sector, organised private sector as well as informal sector in tertiary care, secondary care and even in primary care though in primary care it's not very well organised in terms of providing the care in rural and small towns that we have seen during COVID-19 and indeed we saw during COVID-19 the dependence on the private sector hurt us in India not only were they unable to deliver care in smaller towns and villages but exorbitant rates charged by some of them in urban areas were scandalous and they could not even provide adequate beds for admission and ran short of oxygen supply simply for they were not prepared. That, of course, affected the government sector, which indicated poor governance and preparation of entire sector for public health emergencies.

One of the stark failures of the private sector came into visibility when they were asked to deal with 25% to the vaccines in India and were permitted to acquire 25% vaccines and administer them, we found that beyond few large hospitals in large cities, they could not really deliver more than 7% of the vaccine especially in small towns and villages. So, over-dependency on private sector can be costly for public health and overall efficiency and equity of health care.

We have evolved a mix health care system over the years by default and not by design and therefore, we have to possibly accommodate all the sectors public-private as well as voluntary sectors under a framework of universal health coverage which we need to evolve. But with appropriate regulatory framework and with clearly defined deliverables and accountability mechanism, you cannot have a private sector that is un-regulated or under-regulated and have a completely under-resource public sector having struggle with delivering the care—both vast majority of people who cannot afford health care from out of pocket expenses or particularly deliver most of the services during a public health emergency. So, we need to strengthen our public sector. We need to make our private sector more responsible partner in universal health coverage but with a clear-cut accountability mechanisms and strong regulatory structure.

It requires us to look at the universal health coverage. What is universal health coverage? It is something which is committed to the sustainable development goals which we have incorporated in our National Health Policy of 2017. So, we see that we do require to focus on universal health coverage as a system where every person living in the country gets all the essential health services that he or she needs with assured quality but without suffering financial hardship. That means there should be no high out-of-pocket expenditure, there is no catastrophic expenditure, which should not push them into poverty in emergency or serious health condition.

It appears to be a bit of a tall order because we cannot overnight provide all the services to everybody who needs it immediately unless we raise our public financing of health; while a public financing on health has stagnate to the round 1.4% of the entire gross domestic product (GDP), the government has committed that we must raise it to at least 2.5% of GDP. We possibly will require minimum 3% of GDP in order to deliver reasonable amount of health care services and that is public financing; it can be supplemented by government supported social and health insurance programmes to some extent, employer provided insurance as well as privately purchased insurance. But the bulk of it has to come from the tax funded government exchequer. Without that, we will not be able to maintain our health services at the level of efficiency that it required to deliver all the services.

We recognise that we cannot immediately gather all the resources needed for full-fledged universal health coverage overnight. So, we have to progressively develop that there are three dimensions of universal health coverage, which are described by the World Health Organization. One is population coverage—what proportion of people are being covered by the universal health coverage programme; second is service coverage—what are the services included in the package of services that is provided under universal health coverage which is guaranteed for delivery by the government. But the government is responsible for making sure those services got delivered. The third is what's called cost coverage—how much of the cost of this financing from out of pocket is going to be reduced and how much it is going to be without a financial burden on people. So, cost coverage is important but at the same time you have to make sure that you are spending that money well so that it is not unproductive expenditure or unnecessary procedures and that while reducing poverty levels in the people because of the health care, you are keeping the health budget reasonably under check so that you are not guilty of imprudent financial expenditure.

So, these three aspects have to be balanced. Politicians generally go in for population coverage, because even if the services are few, they like to please many people. The health care providers like doctors would like to go in for a broad service coverage package, because they feel that their patients deserve the best service, however, expensive it is. Whereas, the economists who are usually in the 'Niti Aayog' or Planning Commission as well as the health system managers like health secretary and others, the civil servants, other economists, usually look at the cost coverage and say how much can we actually provide for the universal health coverage packet to provide the maximum benefits possible with the best impact on reducing poverty related to healthcare while keeping the overall budget reasonably under check. So, poverty reduction and fiscal prudence are the guidelines and at any given time, based on the resources available we have to balance all three of them.

It important that we look into the common health conditions which the people mostly suffer from; how do we address those, how do we provide services for that, etc. We also need to look at what is called the equity dimension—which are the vulnerable groups that are the most disadvantaged already, who are suffering from poor health conditions, who are unable to access health services properly because of poverty, disability or because of the variety of other reasons. So, Universal Health Coverage programme has to bring in that dimension to bridge the health equity gaps.

You have two different dimensions—one is what can be called the horizontal equity in which everybody gets the same set of services like primary health care much of secondary health care, lifesaving elements of advanced healthcare but there are groups that will be prioritised for additional resources and additional services to reducing the existing health equity gaps so that would be seen as vertical equity. So we need to balance both of these when we are configuring universal health coverage package. But UHC is the best platform on which we can provide services for many of India's health conditions, right from health promotion about how to build health better so that people don't fall ill to undertaking preventive measures so as to avoid the risks of heart diseases, kidney failures, etc. We also need rehabilitation services and palliative care for people in extreme ends of terminal disease. The health challenges in India are changing; infectious diseases have generally come down over the last three decades. Whereas non-communicable diseases like heart attacks, diabetes, cancer, chronic respiratory disease, mental illness have gone up. It's not that the infectious diseases are completely away, tuberculosis is still a major challenge. So are malaria and dengue, but overall challenges have become less.

We also see huge nutritional challenges. About 38% of the children are still stunted and also under-nourished. Given the huge problem that we see in terms of nutrition deficiency among children, many of our women in the reproductive age group and children under 5 are anaemic. So, we have a problem of under-nutrition, infectious diseases, and chronic diseases like heart diseases, diabetes, cancer, chronic lung diseases. In order to address all of these challenges, we need an efficient health system that is well resourced not only in terms of financing but also in terms of health care delivery services. Of course, technology will help, we should be able to use the health care technology in primary health care to enable the non-doctors like community health worker, nurses, mid-wives and mid-level health care providers for efficiently using technology for delivering services.

But technology alone will not solve the problem; we would still need human resources to use that technology and to connect general health services with advanced health care. This can be done by investing in well trained human resources at different levels. And we must develop our district hospitals and particularly focus on our primary care both in rural areas and in urban areas because, as I said earlier, urban primary health care has been neglected for long—right from sub-centres to primary health care and community health centres. We need continuous care at the primary level for people with long term health problems like diabetes, hyper-tension, etc. We also need connected care where we find that primary care is efficiently connected to secondary care institutions like district hospitals, tertiary care institutions like medical college hospitals and there is referral back to primary care after they have been treated for their immediate health problems.

Unless we establish all of these structures in a seamless manner, we will find people running from pillar to post whenever they have a minor medical problem or a serious medical emergency. We need to reconfigure our health system by re-imagining all of these in a fairly coherent manner. And for that, we need very good public health expertise.

Now, how do you actually configure the health system to make sure that there are enough trained and well-motivated and accountable health care providers at each level of care from sub-centres to district hospitals or to the medical college hospitals. How is the private sector more accountable? How is the public sector to be strengthened so that it can become the pace-setter for high quality healthcare which is affordable to everybody? These are some issues that we ought to be really looking at as we rebuild our health system. And we must ensure that some of these inequalities that exist across our country between rural areas and urban areas, between different states all of them are eliminated.

When we are really looking at re-configuring India and reimagining health system which is much more efficient and equitable, we have to prepare a platform of universal health coverage in order to address all the health challenges and ensure that we build systems which can keep people healthy across their life course but when they do fall ill then we ought to be able to provide them the health care that they required frontally and efficiently. We need better health information systems and for that we need data for early decision making and better governance of a health system by the overall management, right at the policy makers' level to the people who are managing the health care facility. Of course, education is very important, while we improve the education levels of the people, health literacy must be provided with priority. So that people can understand their health and nutrition needs and can take decisions to protect, preserve and promote their health.

All of these are social determinants of health care system and we need to bring that along with the universal health coverage as we rebuild our systems.

Finally, as I said, it's not just building, it is about building forward better by reimagining how an efficient equitable and empathetic health system can be developed. We also need to broaden the community engagement to build better, broader, forward better and fairer. We must focus on health equity as an important criterion of how we configure and deliver our health services.

Journalism

The Journalism You Deserve

Hartosh Singh Bal

My brief today is to speak on the state of the media, and what can be done about it, if anything at all. Before I begin, or delve into the topic, I think it should be clear what we mean by the term media when we use it. I want to distinguish this term from journalism. What is the difference between media and journalism? A journalism is a craft. It is a craft like being a doctor, it's a craft that comes with training, it has its own certain norms and rigour that its practitioners must follow, if they are to do their job honestly. The media is the superstructure that surrounds this craft. In the same way the doctors need hospitals, they need chains, there are owners, there are administrators, that go into forming a medical establishment, journalism is done in a superstructure that we will term media. So, for the purpose of what I am going to be talking about, the media is the superstructure that allows it to journalism. This media consists of, whether it is television studios, newspapers, printing presses, basically media owners, who command and control and fund this whole infrastructure. And, so where does the problem actually lie? The problem that actually infects journalism at its roots is a problem with the media and it often lies outside the practice of journalism itself.

How does the media superstructure in India define itself? Let's just look at some of the organisations that make up the Indian media. Whether you look at a Print in India, English Print, you look at *The Times of India, Hindustan Times, The Indian Express,* you look at the big Hindi newspapers, *Dainik Jagran* and *Dainik Bhaskar*, you look at the channels, you look at *Times Now*, you look at *Republic*, you look at *Aaj Tak,* you look at *India Today,* almost all of them are owned by people drawn from one small community, one small caste. They are largely from the trading castes, and within the trading castes, almost all the ownership is Marwari. What does that imply and what does that mean? What does it mean for this whole superstructure that we have to deal with? This trading caste is, in any case, the caste that largely funded the rise and spread of, what we call Hindutva at the beginning of the 20th century. The printing presses that published the books that uniformised Hinduism, the *Gitas*, the *Ramayana* in published form, that spread across the country were also funded by Marwari businessmen from Kolkata, the same people who actually funded the rise of the Indian media itself, and this same ownership continues today. What is the impact of this ownership? The impact of this ownership is that while we talk of the diversity of media in India, the control of this media lies with a very small group, which with a shared ideology which is largely supportive of the Hindutva that constitutes this country's ruling class at the moment, the Bharatiya Janata Party (BJP) government, as well as the Rashtriya Swayamsevak Sangh (RSS).

The other thing that is quite clear is that when the ownership of the media is drawn from businessman or the business class, they have other interests that tie up with the government. This country actually has a semi-liberalised economy. For any big business to actually work in this country, what does it need? It needs to be on reasonable terms with the government; you still need permissions; you need the government to be on the right side for you to actually spread or propagate your business. What does that mean? That means both financially and ideologically the owners of the media are beholden to the government. In some senses, they are not independent entities in any reasonable fashion. The result of that is that the government can virtually dictate or control what the media does without seeming to be doing so. This is actually evident in all that we see. You see the coverage of the pandemic, you see during the pandemic there was a direct approach by the Prime Minister, Modi himself to the owners, and the owner-editors to broadcast positive news; actually this was largely what was done by the owners and editors. Why do they do it? While, when I spoke of the medical establishment, at doctors at least there the medical establishment has a clear purpose that is to make money, earn money as much as it can. In this case, there are even indirect incentives, that the media also serves as a way to keep the government happy, so the owners of the media can benefit in other ways in other businesses, because many of them own businesses which are far larger than even their media interests.

As a result, that's why we call journalism is restricted by ownership and journalists who actually want to practise their profession in the way they are trained to do so are almost, not just, they find it impossible. It's not as if they are unwilling, most of them are quite willing to take the risks that go with the profession, but they work in structures, and they work and report to people who will not allow them to do this job in the larger part. So what happens with the owners is that the owners are the same people who are appointing editors. If you want to actually find out what a bad journalist is, just look at the editor of a mainstream organisation in India. That would more or less be a bad journalist. The owners are interested only in ensuring bad journalists who do not count out the owners' line, the owners' interests. The owners are the people running these organisations. As a result of mediocrity, that's what defines the media in India. Good journalists want to do their jobs at mid or junior levels, people coming into the profession have to count out to this mediocrity which is in charge of most of these organisations.

This currently is the structure in which journalists operate, there is both at the top level and at the ownership level in ideological complicity, and the second is a financial complicity with the government. So let us not put too much emphasis on the pressures the government puts on the media, that is it arm-twists the media, it forces them to do its bidding, no, the media is complicit in the very actions of the government, because a large part of the media in terms of its ownership and the editors who are appointed, the bad journalists that I've referred to, actually believe in this project of this government and are participants in the bigotry that define this government.

So the question then before us, is that given this kind of superstructure that constrains and defines journalism in this country, what can be done about it? And I do not want to suggest any utopian ideas or solutions. People will talk of different kinds of legislation, norms, ownerships, structures. There will be no change through a legal or legislative means, simply because it is not in the interest of the political class to change the structure of the media. What does that mean? The structure that today the BJP and Modi exploit to their advantage is not a structure they created overnight. The Congress was participant, every opposition party in government was also participant in the same undermining of the structures, or actually encouraging this kind of structure to prosper and proliferate. So, in a real sense there is no political will to actually change this through legislation or through norms that would change the very structure which defines journalism in this country. So, then where is the way out? Large scale utopian solutions do not make sense. There's no point wasting our time about these. The things that can actually work are things that you as individuals, whoever is viewing this, whoever thinks about the media, whoever wants to engage with the media, what is it that any such individual can do? And, the simple fact is that if you look around, if you look around the media today, you look around at how the government is trying to control or divert the media, most of the control or the attempt to clamp down is largely on small media magazines, like the one I work for *The Caravan,* digital portals, *The Wire, Newsclick, Newslaundry, Scroll.*

Why is the government not doing the same thing to mainstream newspapers or channels? Because it doesn't need to. The mainstream has already fallen away. These small organisations that are left survive because the same ownership pressures the same bad journalists which run mainstream newspapers are not represented here. Why do these small magazines or digital portals actually work? They work because they have a direct contact with the people who actually read, view them, or engage with them. There is no money that is coming in from big advertisements, there is no money that is coming from government, that money is coming directly from you. That need for you to invest and look at the media that really works is important, and that choice lies with individuals, people who complain about the media on a large scale in India are deluding themselves if they are not making the choices. What does that mean? If you switch on a mainstream news channel whichever one you want to pick up, *Times Now, Republic*, and then complain about the content you are seeing, you're already making the wrong choice, because a mainstream news channel does not care whether you switch it on to curse it or to praise it. They want eyeballs, they are getting eyeballs. If you are subscribing to any mainstream newspaper, *The Times of India, Hindustan Times*, and you put, pick up, and daily curse that you are not getting news, you are not getting a representative sense of the country, then you are making the wrong choices. You should actually not be going through these newspapers in the morning, because it doesn't matter if you are subscribing to curse, criticise, it really does not matter to the newspaper. What matters is that it is being bought or a channel if it is being bought. So if you do not exercise these choices, you do not actually punish bad journalism, or media houses that are not doing what counts as journalism, then it really doesn't matter what criticism you offer.

In the same way if you do not reward journalism that actually subscribes to the norms of the profession, that follows the checks and balances, then you are actually, again not doing anybody a service. How do you make those choices? First of all, I do not suggest that anybody should be endorsing media or organisations that completely agree with you. This is not an echo chamber. What you have to first look at is, whether the organisations that you turn to, that you are actually investing in journalism from the ground reportage. That is the core of journalism. If you are not getting reportage, if you are not seeing the country represented from across its dimensions, represented in terms of reporting on caste diversity, regional diversity, linguistic diversity, getting reportage from outside the metros, from smaller places, if you're not getting representation of smaller political parties, different political formations, and sometimes this reportage should go against your cherished believes. It is not an echo chamber you are looking for. It should make you question, your assumptions, it should make you examine your beliefs as well. If there is such reportage that is available there, that is the first thing you should support to the extent you can. You are not looking for an endorsement of your personal beliefs in which case you really don't need journalism or media. You are looking for journalism that actually questions the exercise of power, whether that power is exercised by the BJP, or the Congress, by Modi, or an opposition government elsewhere. You cannot simply endorse media that is partisan, that looks only one way. In the current moment, it is necessary that the examination is of BJP, of the ideology of hate that spreads over the country, of Modi itself. But that can only be one large part of the media's job. That to me is the primary concern when you look for organisations. The second thing is that, please, yes you must decide on opinion, look for opinion, but don't make opinion the end all and be all of journalism; of various activists writing and ranting about the government. Do not let that form your idea of journalism; that is a small necessary part, even opinion must be reasoned, it should be backed up by facts, it should be supported by an argument that holds together, it should not simply be about what you like. The third thing is that please ensure that you do not make journalism about individuals. Whether it, first of all, when I say journalism, I'm not counting bloggers, YouTubers, citizen journalists, what I'm counting as are professionally trained people who follow certain norms of veracity, that constitute journalism.

So, while it's good that you may support certain individuals, you may back certain anchors, you may follow certain people with large twitter followings, you may want to look at somebody who has some sub stack, that is not going to, in the end, strengthen journalism or create the kind of media that can actually do what is required in a democracy. You need to look for institutions. It is only when you support and back institutions which grow, and which extend and become powerful enough to look across the country and represent it in its diversity, which then hold up a mirror to the government, which question the exercise of power, only then do we have journalism doing the role it needs to do in democracy. This cannot be done by individuals. Yes, please by any means, after you have looked at institutions, support a journalist here, support a blogger here. It's good, it is good that these exist and these are quick fixes in our time that we do need, but this cannot be the way in which you get a sustainable media environment. Without institutions there is no journalism in the long term, and without this journalistic examination in our country, in the current moment, you will not get accountability of all the other institutions that are supposed to hold the government and to examination.

Today actually we fail to do so, that is quite evident in what is happening around us. The only modes of communication between the government and the electorate, in this country, there are 10 lakh voters for one MP, the only possible communication between the government and the electorate is through journalism. While it is possible for the government to communicate one way through government channels, through propaganda, through advertisement, the only way for the electorate to examine power, to raise questions, to ask what is happening, is through journalism that does its job. Essentially, if what I'm suggesting is not possible, in some senses, we are laying aside India's claim to be a constitutional democracy. Your individual choice, I think, is crucial in this, because this reform is not coming from anywhere outside. It is a structural reform, it will not be done by laws, legislations, legal cases; it will be done by individual choices.

Censorship

Creative Freedom and Censorship

Anand Patwardhan

I have been making films for 50 years. Governments have come and gone and there were difficult experiences with each one in terms of how they responded to our films. Every government tried to interfere with filmmaking in one way or the other, but things have never been worse than they are today. Open public distribution of my films has virtually stopped.

The mechanism for censorship was first created by the British to suppress India's freedom struggle but a modified version was adopted by Independent India. Under previous governments many independent filmmakers like myself still managed to get past the censors. We first went through different stages in the Central Board of Film Certification (CBFC, known as the Censor Board) comprising various revising committees and finally, the appellate tribunal, a high level body with an ex-judge who would look at remaining grievances. Now they have removed the appellate tribunal.

When all remedies within CBFC including the appellate tribunal failed, I went to court. Fighting censorship has a long legal history in India. Because the Indian Constitution respects the right to freedom of expression, there are many landmark judgments in court, like the judgment on K A Abbas's film *A Tale of Four Cities* (1968) which ruled that a filmmaker had the right to depict existing poverty even if it embarrassed the government, or the judgment on Govind Nihalani's *Tamas* (1988) which reiterated that censors must imagine an audience of reasonable people and not worry about a few malcontents who might take offence. When I went to court I could quote from these judgments in defence of my own work. We even went to court to force Doordarshan, our national broadcaster, to show my films whenever any had won a National Award. With the unstinting help of my pro bono lawyers PA Sebastian in the Bombay High Court and Nitya Ramakrishnan and Prashant Bhushan in the Supreme Court, we argued that if a government can award a film, surely the film must be viewable by the public, and so the national broadcaster must show it. We won seven cases in all and twice the judge ordered the films to be shown at prime time. Today it's difficult to achieve the same.

Constitutional bodies like the Central Board of Film Certification (CBFC) apart, there is also the censorship of the mob. Goondas or extra-constitutional vigilantes who do not like what a film is saying, riot and disturb or terrorise exhibitors into abandoning the screening. Mob censorship has occasionally afflicted fiction film releases. It has happened multiple times to my film *Ram Ke Naam*, in different locations like Law College in Pune, Ambedkar University in Delhi, Hyderabad Central University, Presidency University, Kolkata to name just a few. In some of these cases the film screening could still go ahead because there was a censor certificate and legally, they could not stop it. In Delhi for example, students called in the police and finally the goonda elements were thrown out. Shockingly the government is now trying to bring in a new amendment that will allow them to remove censor certificates granted by previous governments. The amendment if promulgated will allow the present regime to simply withdraw censor certificates granted earlier. Film screenings would then become illegal and they could bust into a screening, confiscate equipment and even put you in jail for showing a film without a newer certificate.

I don't think many democratic countries resort to such extreme interference in film making, especially of documentary films. Of course fiction is also subject to censorship but here the cuts they ask for have mainly to do with sex and violence. In fact, violence bothers them less than sex. Many Bollywood films celebrate violence. With documentary films the main censorship is political. Criticism of the government or of the government's ideology is not tolerated. Things are worse if you have a secular ideology today. In other words, if your ideology is actually in consonance with our Constitution, then right now you are in deep trouble. In my view the present government is constitutional only in the sense that it was elected but it clearly does not follow the spirit of the Constitution. So, when you do follow the spirit of the Constitution, you fall afoul of what the government thinks you are allowed to do. Steadily the government has increased both its desire for, and its ability to, control. The index of democracy has fallen dramatically and we are at a very low rank in the world in terms of freedom of expression. Every institution of the government is now tuned to crush dissent.

We denounce groups like ISIS and Taliban but I don't think extreme right-wing Hindutva supremacists are very different. Yet the last 9 years of BJP rule has given unfettered freedom and institutional support to them. What is different from the Emergency of 1975 is that today's Emergency has not been officially declared. Democracy exists only in theory and only for certain sections. The targets earmarked for repression are focussed so the bulk of the middle and elite classes do not realise there is an Emergency-like situation around them because today's targets are not the elite. Those targeted are the weakest sections among Muslims, Christians, Dalits and all who organise the working classes.

Institutions are being systematically compromised and dissent is not tolerated. In the days I was growing up and went to college we could protest against situations we felt were wrong. Now even the physical space for protest has narrowed. Now there are designated sites where people can go protest—like a Jantar Mantar in Delhi or a tiny section of the 'Azad' Maidan in Mumbai. Earlier we could protest almost anywhere and it was taken notice of by the media. Today the mainstream media, bought by crony capital, largely ignores incidents of protest. If at all they do cover it, the extent is controlled by the government, and a majoritarian plant, thinly disguised as a 'political analyst' gets to add his or her spin. Up to a year ago despite such controls someone like a Ravish Kumar still managed to do decent reporting and analysis, and the government could not get *NDTV* to fire him. So they went one better and got their biggest crony capitalist, Gautam Adani, to buy out the channel. Today *NDTV* has become a joke, much more tragic than funny.

Battles against censorship have been fought outside court as well. The Mumbai International Film Festival (MIFF) never asked for censor certificates when it first began in 1991. It is an international documentary film festival and films from all over the world were never asked for censor certificates. In 2002 an anti-Muslim pogrom had taken place in Gujarat under the watch of Chief Minister Modi. The BJP was in power at the Centre. Fearing critical films, a rule was introduced that required Indian films at the festival to have censor certificates. Outraged Indian filmmakers ran a parallel festival called Vikalp. We were soon joined by international filmmakers and we showed films regardless of certificates and our festival attracted bigger crowds than the official one. Of course, this was at a relatively early stage of BJP rule and we could get away with it. Since then groups like Vikalp have mushroomed across the country.

Social media and OTT platforms are a bit of relief in present times. But this is not an ideal situation because individuals watching a small computer monitor or phone is no substitute for a big screen with a live audience. We used to screen our films and have discussions with large audiences but that has become rare. Social media is also controlled. In the early days of Facebook, each of my posts would get 60,000 or more views and these were growing all the time. Then Facebook monetised, changed algorithms, and now if lucky, I get few hundred views. Any content which is critical of the government immediately gets restricted. Even on YouTube, my films for which we fought hard to get a 'U' certificates have been restricted with dire false alarms about their content. Several other methods like fake copyright strikes are employed to restrict the reach of any content critical of the powers that be.

We all know what happened to Twitter. Twitter tried to stand up to the government, the government cracked down on them. The so-called 'international' social media is also controlled either directly through the government or its majoritarian ideologues who infest Silicon valley. On OTT platforms like Netflix, our last film *Reason* which won Best Feature at the International Documentary Film Festival in Amsterdam and qualified for the Oscar race, could easily have been shown as an eight-part serial but Netflix told me openly that if they showed the film, they would be thrown out of India. Oscar nominated Indian documentaries like *Writing with Fire* and *All that Breathes* were not shown out of the same fear. Even Meera Nair's *A Suitable Boy* ran into trouble because bigots started making a noise about the Hindu-Muslim romance in it. Luckily the film was not taken off but the noise reached everybody and Netflix in particular. Such censorship is specially harmful to people who make high budget films and have a lot to lose if their avenues are suddenly cut off. Most content producers end up doing self-censorship and playing it safe. In our case it doesn't matter so much as big distribution channels have been closed to us for a long time.

We continue doing what we believe in. These circumstances will not last forever. Everything changes and we must keep moving forward. If we censor ourselves we send out a message of fear. So we will keep speaking. And keep finding ways to get the word out.

S4/078/F